CAPON VALLEY
Sampler

CAPON VALLEY
Sampler

Sketches of Appalachia
from George Washington to Caudy Davis

Willard Wirtz

Bartleby Press

Silver Spring, Maryland

Printed in the United States of America

Published and Distributed by:

Bartleby Press
11141 Georgia Avenue
Silver Spring, Maryland 20902
(301) 949-2443

Library of Congress Cataloging-in-Publication Data

Wirtz, Willard, 1912-
  Capon Valley sampler : sketches of Appalachia from George Washington to Caudy Davis / Willard Wirtz.
    p. cm.
  ISBN 0-910155-14-3
  1. Cacapon River Valley (W. Va.)—History. 2. Cacapon River Valley (W. Va.)—Social life and customs. 3. Yellow Spring Region (W. Va.)—History. 4. Yellow Spring Region (W. Va.)—Social life and customs. 5. Davis, Caudy George, 1886-1985. 6. Wirtz, Willard, 1912- .   I. Title.
F247.C24W57   1990   89-29144
975.4′93—dc20   CIP

For Jane, partner in the
adventure we call Tannery

Contents

Preface

A sampler, as I understand needlework's term, makes no pretenses. An amateur experimenting with different stitches tries to be careful but doesn't worry about whether the designs fit together. The point of each exercise is largely in the satisfaction of doing it.

So of this little volume. While its sketches relate in various ways to the life and times of Yellow Spring, West Virginia, a small two-and-a-half-century-old community in the Cacapon Valley that gave new life to a pair of political refugees from Washington, D.C., no story develops. What is here reflects the pleasure a congenital scribbler finds in sitting down once in a while at a desk with a pad of paper, a pen, and a few hours that don't have to be accounted for.

My original thought was to try to write the story of a remarkable man, Caudy Davis, Yellow Spring patriarch and, in a sense, our patron here. An essentially private man, he encouraged making the story less about him than about the community. He warned that there wouldn't be many records to rely on.

Mister Caudy was right. Some of these pieces depend heavily on casual talks I had with him and with neighbors whose families have been part of this community for four or five, sometimes six or seven, generations. After experimenting with a tape recorder, it seemed better, a smaller threat to the conversations, to make a few notes as we chatted and then to flesh them out as soon as I got home. If reliance on this hand-me-down hearsay has resulted in occasional minor fractures of fact I don't believe that essential truths have suffered serious injury.

Although nothing here is my own invention, I haven't written under oath. This is storytelling country, and well-spun yarns or pregnant anecdotes have seemed worth reporting, if they appeared even mildly plausible, without cross-examination. But where warts showed up I usually left them out, and when a glimpse into a closet met a skeletal stare I closed the door—except in the case of the ballot box stuffing of 1862. Yellow Spring's wart-and-hidden-skeleton average is probably about like Washington's, which doesn't deserve the unequal time it gets in the papers and on television.

Part of the sampler exercise has been to try to put things in a form that comes closest to meeting both Capon Valley tastes and more cosmopolitan interests. If some details that might distract strangers to Yellow Spring have been included, quite a few more of considerable local importance have been left out. As far as "elements of style" are concerned, *The New Yorker*'s E.B. White and John Ailes, editor of the local *Hampshire Review*, would agree, and so do I, that fewer words are better than more, that one or two syllables have an advantage over four or five, and that stranded prepositions and sundered infinitives are less to be pitied than are jaded metaphors and bedridden cliches.

It means a great deal to me that Arlene Huff has been a partner in this undertaking. We worked together in side-by-side offices for most of twenty-five years. Her secretarial assistance, including typing redrafts of the Sampler, has been only the superficial part of her always selfless contribution to our common enterprises, professional, political, and most of all personal.

Finally, Jane and I are as large creditors as our Yellow Spring neighbors and friends will ever have. One of the community's customs is that few thank yous are ever said. But almost everybody contributes something or other, whatever is possible, to a common fund of caring and sharing. It is pleasant to think of this weaving together of some threads of the Yellow Spring story as a grateful effort to put my kind of handiwork beside the rest.

W.W.
Yellow Spring, W. Va.
1990

Escape to Reality

Jane and I first met "the old Davis place" on a crisp, sun-flooded October morning in 1967. A long lane led up from the Cacapon River past a few cows grazing in a pasture, toward a time-grayed frame house set at the base of a modest mountainside vivid with aspen yellows and maple reds. White smoke curled up gracefully from the chimney. It was the kind of setting West Virginians have in mind when they claim on bumper stickers their Almost Heaven copyright.

But then we came to the gate across the lane in front of the house. Propped in place and tied shut with binder twine, clearly serving no purpose in a fence whose broken pickets had lost all sense of duty, the wood curtain's message was blunt. If the old Davis place was for sale, which we had been warned was uncertain, somebody was opposing the notion.

Caudy Davis, a senior member of the family who was showing us the property, handled the situation with seasoned equanimity. Turning the car around and stopping only briefly while we looked at the house, which revealed from this closer vantage point signs of structural arthritis, he was matter of fact. "A few things need doing." Then he shifted the conversation. "You may be interested that the center part of the house is a two-story log cabin. Built in the late eighteenth century, in 1794 I think. And the property was surveyed by George Washington." We smiled. So did he, "No, I can't say whether he slept here or not."

Driving back down the lane, we crossed the river by a shallow ford and then followed service tracks up a hill to a pasture that commands a view several miles up and down the Capon Valley. Three deer, grazing at the edge of the clearing, watched us for a minute or so and then did their ballerina exits, white tail-flags bobbing, over the fence and into the pines.

Driving back the seven miles to the Capon Springs Hotel, where we were staying, Mister Caudy—as Ted Austin from the hotel called him, pronouncing it "Coddy"—explained the problem we had encountered at the gate. The property belonged to Caudy's older brother Tom, who had recently moved up the river to live with one of his daughters. The family was "undecided" about what to do with the homeplace. A son was still living there.

Mister Caudy asked us whether we were interested in the property. We said we were.

"Would you be moving here?"

We explained our situation. Having decided after seven years in Washington not to go back to Illinois, we wanted to find a weekend escape hatch from official pressures—"or from too many Republicans if they take over." Mister Caudy smiled approvingly; we knew from Ted's report that at one point in his life he had served as a delegate—Democratic—in the West Virginia legislature.

When we got out at the hotel he asked whether we would care to see the house some time. I had begun to realize that our host was doing as much inspecting that morning as his guests were; we had apparently passed the test. When we said yes to his offer, he indicated that it could be arranged for the following weekend.

This time the gate was open. No one was in the house. It turned out to be more ample than had appeared from the outside. The log cabin part is one large room on each floor, with three others having been added upstairs and down at the back and on one side. Although we found more effects of age than we had expected, we knew—and indicated—that if the Davises were interested, so were the Wirtzes.

The weeks, which became months, of conversations that followed were a lesson in both Capon Valley values and the local pace of doing business, especially when land is involved. Price wasn't a problem. The asking (and closing) figure for "160 acres more or less" of improved West Virginia farm and woodland with quite a stretch of river front was almost exactly what we had received recently for our modest home on a half-acre lot in Winnetka, on Chicago's North Shore. We shook our heads about contemporary civilization's strange mixing up of land and status price tags.

A more critical passage involved a telephone call from Mister Caudy about whether we would object to some other Davises and their friends hunting on the property during deer season, the two weeks in November that mean more to the men here than all the rest of the year. Thinking of those three graceful creatures soaring over the fence at the edge of the pasture, we hesitated but agreed.

As one question after another came up, we began to sense the trauma that builds up in the valley around selling property. People here have been so close to the soil for so long, the same families on the same places, drawing their living from the earth, that land and man (woman in a different way) have become almost one. In local usage you don't talk about hunting on John Kline's property but about "hunting on John." The Tom Davis property had been in the family for 130 years. Despite our political empathy with Caudy Davis, others in the family perhaps took particular objection to selling to Washington bureaucrats, local shorthand for meddlers in other people's business.

Whatever the problem in the family was got resolved by our agreeing to accept title without guarantee of immediate possession. Everything finally worked out and we spent our first weekend here in May of 1968.

We knew that our title deed was only a passport and that membership in the local community, which is called Yellow Spring, wasn't for sale. So we worked at it. Yet it came as a gift, generously given. I think this was after our neighbors, Willetta Davis and Tootie Kline, learned that Jane makes all her own clothes and knows as many recipes as they do.

It might have been easier if I could have taken a normal masculine interest in deer hunting. There was also a setback when I tried to help Forrest Davis (Tom and Caudy's nephew) corner a cow that was having trouble with a breech delivery of her calf; slipping on a common barnyard land mine in the pasture, I fell on my face and the cow sailed on by. But we finally got to her, and with Forrest holding her down on her side (which I couldn't manage) and providing the necessary instructions, I reached in, released the calf's hind leg, and then added a little pulling to Mrs. Angus's anguished delivery. Her eventual success was a moment of ultimate achievement for both of us.

I expect it helped that we didn't try to fancy the house up, and that we did as much of the necessary repair work as we could ourselves. Charley Alger, local carpenter-painter-plumber-plasterer extraordinary, made a few minor changes and restored the sagging two-tiered front porches to life. When it came to reviving the picket fence, to establish an equal but separate relationship with the small herd of cattle, Forrest Davis and his sons Dwight and Guy cut two pine trees and a locust across the river, took the timber to John Brill's sawmill, brought back the necessary posts and stringers and picket stock, and then insisted on doing most of the work on the fence themselves—especially after they realized that I didn't know enough to spit on a nail so that it could be driven without bending into a locust post. (I managed to maintain this strictly amateur status by driving the Scout into a four-foot drainage ditch, burning out the element in the electric water heater, and dowsing a fire in the ashtray of the car with antifreeze fluid marked inflammable on the can.)

Spending only weekends here during 1968 (it's a two-hour drive from Washington), we moved in on a temporary full-time basis after the Republican occupation of the nation's capital the following January. There was a lot to do. Although quite a bit of furniture had come with the house, we went almost every Saturday to local estate auctions, usually bringing back in-the-rough pieces that required considerable attention. I stripped the old paint or varnish, and Jane did the refinishing. She conjured up curtains and cushions and

screens while I scraped four layers of paint and white-
wash off the upstairs ceiling and re-chinked the logs.
The only real strain developed when we papered one
of the bedrooms with a small flowered design that demanded more careful matching than a pair of novices
should have attempted. It was a vintage year.

Although the name "the old Davis place" survives
unscathed in local usage, we also call the property Tannery. When he came here in 1839, Samuel Davis, Tom
and Caudy's grandfather, put in equipment a hundred
yards north of the house for tanning cowhide. This was
his occupation, along with farming, until after what
is called locally the War Between the States. Samuel's
sons, and then their's, including Tom, continued the
tanning business until the 1920s. The machinery from
the old tannery still keeps its vigil beside the pond that
the Forrest Davises and we put in together, crossing
our common property line, in 1970.

If Tannery takes its name and a good deal of its
character from the family that has lived here for so
long, two other shaping forces warrant recognition.
One is the river that carved this valley and gave it
tranquil beauty. The other is a community that has
somehow managed to preserve human values planted
here two centuries ago.

The Cacapon is the least known of the four principal
tributaries that flow into the Potomac from the south.
The Shenandoah ("Daughter of the Stars" among the
Algonquins) is familiar in American history, literature, and song. The Blue Ridge Mountains and North
Mountain, whose crest marks the boundary line between Virginia and West Virginia, separate the Shenandoah from the Cacapon valley. Twenty miles farther

west and beyond three modest mountain ranges, the South Branch (once the Wappatomaca—with either a "c" or a "k") flows past Petersburg, Moorefield, and Romney. The westernmost of the four tributaries, the North Branch, has recently been memorialized by Gilbert Gude in his sensitive and delightful *Where the Potomac Begins,* published in 1984.

The Cacapon is a born-again river that leads a double life under two names. Rising from a small cluster of springs near West Virginia's eastern edge, "Lost River" moves generally north for twenty miles or so, becoming a lovely rock-studded trout stream. Then, encountering Sandy Ridge, the river solves its problem—and picks up its name—by disappearing into a hole in the ground. The same waters re-emerge on the other side of the ridge as the "Cacapon." Proceeding another fifty miles up the map, which seems against nature, the river enters the Potomac near Berkeley Springs, about midway between Harpers Ferry, West Virginia, and Cumberland, Maryland.

The valley that the Cacapon and Lost rivers have formed winds between softly contoured Oriskany sandstone mountain ridges thickly upholstered with oak, walnut, aspen, locust, maple, and pine. Part of nature's artistry here is a built-in protection against the customary defilements of progress. There is no coal in this part of the state. The valley is fertile but wide enough for only small family farms. The water, too shallow most of the year for even an outboard motor, is crystal clear and pure. Although this ribbon of quiet beauty was included in the Wild and Scenic Rivers Act of 1968, local sentiment against "the Feds," rooted in memories of revenuers invading the privacy of homemade stills back of the barn and up in the hollows, re-emerged so strongly in opposition to the government's conservation plans that the authorities decided not to pursue the statute's benevolent intent.

According to various reports, the Indians called the river Cacapahaowen, Calapechan, or Caor-Capon, said to have meant "medicine running water," "fierce running stream" (which seems dubious), "beautiful waters," or "to be found again." Early white settlers called it the Great Cacapehon. Strangers pronounce the present name Cac-a-pon; people living here, when they go to that much trouble, say Ca-ca-pon. The common "Capon" contraction adds a mildly distracting barnyard overtone to whatever the Indians may have had in mind.

Ten miles below Sandy Ridge, the river comes to the small community that is announced by two road signs about 400 yards apart on State Route 259 as "Yellow Springs, Unincorporated." Unless passing motorists honor the modest request to slow down to forty-five miles an hour, they don't notice the several buildings along the highway: a general store, an automobile service station and parts shop, the grain mill, and eight or ten houses. The "Yellow Spring" post office, where 150 or so families pick up their mail, is in a new wing of the service station.

Kenneth Seldon runs the general store, his son David the service station. David's wife Peggy is the postmaster; not mistress, thank you just the same. The mill has been owned and operated by three generations of Davises, ever since Caudy and his brother Carson bought it in 1914. The post office, garage, and mill are closed for an hour at noon while their keepers go home for lunch.

The community's name, including an enduring uncertainty about whether it is singular or plural, comes from either one or both of two springs several hundred feet up the mountainside. One seeps out timidly through a vein of ochre rock, bringing to the surface a little sediment of yellow sand. The other, gushing strong and clear, is piped down to supply local needs; its flow once turned the thirty-foot iron wheel on the side of the grain mill. Because the plural "Yellow Springs" is more common locally, I started using it. When Jane dissented, we put the matter to Caudy Davis, who issued his decree without even hearing my case. "It's Yellow Spring, of course. Always has been." And so it is here.

A Certain Tract of Waste Land

Capon Valley custom is not to question a good story, especially after it reaches a respectable age. Caudy Davis had told us that the log cabin part of our house has eighteenth-century seniority and that our metes and bounds were laid out by George Washington. By Yellow Spring standards these attractive and plausible ideas were entitled to full faith and credit.

So Mister Caudy was a little taken aback when I asked him one day if he knew where I could find the Washington records. His answer was almost abrupt. "You can't. That was an early survey—about 1750, maybe a year or two before." He went on to explain that this was part of Virginia and that Hampshire County, which now includes the Yellow Spring area, hadn't yet been established. The early records, kept in Richmond, were lost, probably burned, when the British took over the colonial capital during the Revolutionary War. But we arranged to drive over to Romney, the Hampshire county seat, to check the records there.

It was a rewarding trip. Mister Caudy, a surveyor once himself, knew how to use the Hampshire Deed Books. The early volumes are written in longhand on time-yellowed pages, but are remarkably readable once you adjust to the letter s written like an f.

We moved quickly from one volume to another following the title line of the old Davis place back to its coming into the family in 1839, when Tom and Caudy's grandfather Samuel Davis acquired it from one Joel Ellis. The Ellis purchase had been in 1817 from a William Parrill, who had inherited it in 1809 from his father John. In the earliest volume of the Hampshire Deed Books, we came finally to a 1794 deed to John Parrill from a Joseph Steele. There are several Parrill documents, and they make it fairly clear that the cabin that is here now, in modified form, was indeed put up in the 1790s, probably about the time of the 1794 deed. This was precisely what Mister Caudy had told us.

So he smiled a little wearily when I agreed that this established the cabin's antiquity but not the distinction of the property's reputed surveyor. Turning back to the Steele-to-Parrill deed, he pointed to a recital in it that the tract was part of the original holding of "the late Lord Fairfax, proprietor of the Northern Neck of Virginia."

"You know of course," Mister Caudy said, knowing of course that I knew nothing of the sort, "that George Washington was Lord Fairfax's surveyor."

Which should probably have closed the matter. Neither Jane nor I would be inclined to attach anything more than passing conversational value to George Washington's sleeping, surveying, or otherwise conducting himself here. But I enjoy puzzles and this looked like a good one. If Caudy Davis was right, what was the father of American independence doing in the service of a British nobleman? Who was this Fairfax, whose name is so common in Virginia history, and where did he get his entitlement to whatever was meant by the Northern Neck? So I set out on a pursuit that has proved no less pleasant for its triviality.

It won't affect local land values materially that the first "owner" of river frontage along the Cacapon turns out to have been, in the eyes of white man's law, Sir Walter Raleigh. Raleigh's entitlement came by way of a formal grant from Queen Elizabeth, and hers in turn from that allegedly divine right that is spelled out in neither the Old nor the New Testament. Telling this story in detail, Winchester historian Oren Frederic Morton comments on "the propensity of English monarchs for giving away land that didn't belong to them."

Morton and others have reported on Raleigh's receiving from his queen, in 1583, a patent to sail to America and "to inhabit and possess . . . all remote and heathen lands not in actual possession of any Christian prince." Raleigh's emissaries, two seafaring captains, Philip Amadas and Arthur Barlowe, arrived at Bodie Island, off what is now the North Carolina coastline, on July 13, 1584, moving on after a few days to Roanoke Island.

Setting sail again two months later and arriving safely in London, the two captains were received with acclaim. Delighted with the reported discovery of "the part of the country now called Virginia, anno 1584," Queen Elizabeth knighted Raleigh and granted him all property within 600 miles of Roanoke Island. The

Cacapon Valley is well within that radius, which neither its new owner nor his queen may have realized
clearly at the time.

Raleigh's venture subsequently aborted. Despite his
sending another expedition to Roanoke in 1586, its sad
sequel was the "Lost Colony," of which all remnants
have disappeared in history's haze. When Queen Elizabeth died in 1602, her successor, James I, sharing
none of the queen's regard for Raleigh, clapped him in
prison, kept him there for fifteen years, and then had
him beheaded. The first formal title line to property
in the "remote and heathen" Cacapon Valley ended in
a pool of blood in the Tower of London.

King James's own grants of similar patents in 1606
to two groups of promoters, the London Company and
the Plymouth Company, also came to nothing of significance. Arriving in America, the companies' explor-
ers worked their way up the Petomek (the
Cohongorutum in one Indian dialect—today the Potomac) and the river they christened James after their
royal patron. But they stayed in the tidewater area,
never crossing the ridges covered with a purple haze
which the Indians called the Quirauk or Quiranh and
believed were the abode of evil and jealous spirits.
These "Blue Ridge Mountains" are about twenty miles
east of the Cacapon.

Looking into these first two exercises of divine
right as interpreted by British royalty had contributed
nothing to solving the riddle of Who Surveyed What
Along the Cacapon. A third line of inquiry was to prove
more promising. It started with the record of a 1664
grant by Charles II to seven of his favored subjects,
one of them a Lord John Culpeper. The grant covered

"the Northern Neck of Virginia," which was described as including "all land lying between the Potomac and the Rappahannock Rivers." Although this was probably meant to apply only to land east of the Blue Ridge, Culpeper and his associates argued that their western boundary was a line drawn between the headwaters of the two rivers. This would extend the grant to cover six million acres, including the Cacapon Valley.

Nothing came of either the grant or the argument for eighty years. John Culpeper and his son Thomas eventually picked up the interests of the other six grantees, and then the rights passed on Thomas's death to his daughter Catherine. She married Thomas Fairfax, Fifth Baron of Cameron, and in 1717 the Northern Neck became the property of Thomas and Catherine's son—also Thomas, aged twenty-five.

It was a broken arrow from cupid's bow that finally brought this paper title line to life. For reasons history has forgotten, young Thomas Fairfax, now Sixth Baron of Cameron, was jilted by the woman he was engaged to marry. It left him, in historian Morton's description, "a bachelor to the end of his life, with an unyielding aversion to the other sex," and in the 1730s, his Lordship fled from sorrow and bitterness by coming to Virginia to exploit his six million acres.

Fairfax had engaged his cousin William as land agent, and William had built a palatial mansion, which he called Belvoir, on the lower Potomac, just above where it enters Chesapeake Bay. William's daughter had married Major Lawrence Washington. Their estate, called Mt. Vernon, was next door to Belvoir. A frequent visitor there, coming over from his home at Ferry Farm, in Westmoreland County, was Major Washington's considerably younger half-brother, George.

The pieces of the puzzle were beginning to fit together.

Although the Sixth Baron of Cameron fared well by collecting annual fees from settlers in the area near Belvoir, he became alarmed at what was happening on the holdings he claimed west of the Blue Ridge. Starting in the 1720s, settlers had moved into the area from the north, crossing the Potomac and pushing south along its tributaries. By the middle 1730s, a community of "about sixty houses, rather poorly built" had been established at what was called Frederick Town (now Winchester).

Two of these settlers, Joist Hite and James Wood, had gone to Richmond and persuaded the colonial authorities there to grant them title to large tracts of land in and around Frederick Town—on the theory that the 1664 grant to Culpeper and his associates extended west only to the Blue Ridge. Disputing this claim, Fairfax established a local base at a hunting lodge he called Greenway Court, at White Post near Stephensburg (now Stephens City), about ten miles east of Frederick Town.

The degree of strain that developed along the Fairfax/Wood-Hite axis is suggested in historian Samuel Kercheval's account—in his classic 1833 *History of the Valley of Virginia*—of his Lordship's effort to transplant the Frederick County Court, of which Wood was clerk, from Frederick Town to Stephensburg, which was Fairfax's headquarters:

> Tradition relates that Fairfax used all of his influence to make Stephensburg the seat of Justice, but that Wood out-generaled his Lordship, and by treating one of the justices with a bowl of toddy secured his vote in

favor of Winchester, which settled the question, and that Fairfax was so offended at the magistrate who thus sold his vote, that he never after spoke to him.

Spurned in London and rejected in Frederick Town, Fairfax pursued relentlessly his claim to the millions of acres of the Northern Neck lying west of the Blue Ridge. He faced two obstacles. In addition to the dispute about the interpretation of the 1664 grant from King Charles, there was the difficulty that under the 1732 Treaty of Albany, the colonists had agreed with the Indian tribes not to push white settlements beyond the Blue Ridge.

Fairfax finally succeeded. The Treaty of Lancaster, worked out with the Indians in 1744, moved the limit on European settlement fifty miles west to the Alleghenies. And a year later a court decision extended the western boundary of Fairfax's Northern Neck claims to the line drawn between the Potomac and Rappahannock headwaters.

In 1746 and 1747, he and Wood and Hite worked out an accommodation. Dividing up the Frederick Town acreage, with Wood and Hite taking most of it, they agreed that Fairfax would be recognized as proprietor of the territory west of the town. This included the Cacapon and Wappatomaca valleys. In 1753, the Virginia Assembly formalized this agreement by separating these valleys from Frederick County and making them Hampshire County.

Fairfax lost no time in going after the squatters who had infested the western reaches of his Northern Neck. He hired James Genn, an experienced surveyor, to make an initial swing through part of the territory as early in the spring of 1748 as the weather permitted, and before the leafing out of the trees made surveying difficult.

Genn needed assistance, and Fairfax had it available for him. George Fairfax, son of his Lordship's agent (and cousin) William Fairfax, wanted to make the trip. So, it turned out, did neighbor Major Lawrence Washington's brother George.

The sixteen-year-old Washington boy was specially qualified for membership in the party. In his view, which his mother did not fully share, he had just completed his formal education. He had done particularly well in arithmetic, and because the principal of the Academy in Westmoreland County, where George took his schooling, had added surveying and navigation to the curriculum, George had gotten into both of these pursuits. He leaned toward going to sea, but here again his mother had reservations which may or may not have contributed to George's turning instead to surveying. He entered in one of his copybooks a thirty-eight-page course of study entitled "The Art of Surveying and Measuring of Land," and only a few days before the matter of the Genn surveying party came up, George had demonstrated his skills by laying out a plat of "Major Law. Washington's Turnip Field" which he included in his copybook, dated February 27, 1748 and signed "Survey'd by me. . . . G.W."

Surveyor Genn and his two assistants left Belvoir on March 11, 1748, came out to Frederick Town, rode over to the Potomac and then up to the South Branch, where they surveyed a number of lots. They spent two weeks in what would become Hampshire County.

Although historians differ about how much actual surveying the Tory landlord's young acquaintance did on this trip, larger importance lies in the fact that the sixteen-year-old kept a day-to-day diary in a small 5″ × 3¼″ vellum-bound notebook which he carried in his pocket. Including the metes and bounds of the several dozen tracts that were surveyed, he added each night some personal observations on the day's events. The journal, now in the Library of Congress in Washington, was brilliantly edited "with literal exactness and . . . notes" in 1892 by Dr. J. M. Toner, under the title *Journal of My Journey Over the Mountains; by George Washington, While Surveying for Lord Thomas Fairfax, Baron of Cameron.*

This fascinating document proceeds unrestrained by any conventions of spelling, punctuation, capitalization, or grammar. The entry for Tuesday, March 15, 1748, is typical:

> We set out early with Intent to Run round ye sd Land but being taken in a Rain & it Increasing very fast obliged us to return, it clearing about one o'Clock & our time being too Precious to Loose we a second time ventured out & Worked hard till Night & then return'd to Penningtons we got our Suppers & was Lighted into a Room & I not being so good a Woodsman as ye rest of my Company striped myself very orderly & went in to ye Bed as they called it when to my Surprise I found it to be nothing but a Little Straw Matted together without Sheets or anything else but only one thread Bear blanket with double its Weight of Vermin such as Lice Fleas &c I was glad to get up (as soon Y Light was carried from us) I put on my cloths & Lay as my Companions. Had we not been very tired I am sure we should not have slep'd much that night I made a Promise not to Sleep so from that night forward chusing rather to sleep in y. open Air before a fire. . . .

For the following day:

We set out early & finish'd about one oClock & then Travell'd up to Frederick Town where our Baggage came to us we cleaned ourselves (to get rid of y. Game we had catched y. Night before).

Washington's impression of some of the settlers who had entered the Northern Neck was recorded in his journal entry for Monday, April 4th, when the party was surveying along the Wappatomaca (now the South Branch, about twenty miles west of the Cacapon):

We did two Lots & was attended by a great Company of People Men Women & Children that attended us through ye Woods as we went showing there Antick tricks I really think they seem to be as Ignorant a Set of People as the Indians they would never speak English but when spoken to they speak all Dutch.

Yet however much young George's journal may add to the story of the making of a young nation's first president, it cast a serious cloud on Caudy Davis's accuracy as a reporter of local history. While confirming that Washington did some apprentice surveying in this general area in 1748, close enough in time to Mister Caudy's "1750, maybe a year or two before," the journal's only Capon Valley reference is in the entry for Sunday, April 10th: "We took our farewell of ye Branch [the Wappatomaca] and travell'd over Hills and Mountains to I. Coddys on Great Cacapehon about 40 Miles." The next day: "We travell'd from Coddy's down to Frederick Town"—on the way back to Belvoir.

The "I. Coddy" was Washington's minor corruption of "James Caudy." The Caudy cabin, where the surveying party slept that one night, was twelve miles down the river from what would become, nearly a century later, the Davis place at Yellow Spring. Settler

Caudy's namesake seemed to have taken a yarn spinner's license with factual details.

The story was to have another chapter though. And then one more.

Young Washington came back from his trip with Genn intent on getting himself credentialed as a surveyor, which he did in remarkably, even suspiciously, short order. Philander Chase, Associate Editor of *The Papers of George Washington*, has pieced the story together in his 1989 monograph *George Washington as Backcountry Surveyor and Landholder*. The first step was getting a commission as surveyor from the President and Masters of the College of William and Mary, which involved none of the actual matriculation this implies, but obligated the surveyor to pay one-sixth of his fees to the college—which Washington, following established custom, ignored. In July of 1749, he was formally appointed to the post of County Surveyor of the newly created Culpeper County. These county offices were posts that experienced surveyors vied for, and editor Chase leaves no question but that novice Washington's extraordinary advancement was arranged for by Fairfax—who owned the land that constituted the new county.

After laying out several tracts in the Culpeper area, Washington came in November of 1749 to Greenway Court to help Fairfax catch up with the settlers who had come, without license, onto the lands determined to belong to Fairfax in the 1745 court decree. Washington brought with him as his chainman one John Lonem, apparently from the Belvoir area.

The crew started near the headwaters of Lost River. The first tract they surveyed, on November 1, 1749, was for Edward Hogan: "a certain Tract of Waste and

Ungranted Land Situate Lying and being . . . on the Lost River or Cacapehon about Six Miles within the Boundary Line of the Northern Neck." Washington entered this description in his field book, which was about the size he had used for his journal, and then added the boundary descriptions: "Beginning at a white Oak and white Pine Saplins on the West Side of the River and Runs thence S° 68° E Two Hundred and Eighty Poles to three Chestnut Oaks on a Steep Mountain Side. . . ." These field notes were taken back to Greenway Court and used as the basis for drawing up detailed plats and eventually formal grants.

Washington and Lonem worked rapidly. Moving down the valley, they laid out fourteen more tracts during the next ten days, the last of them for William Warden—in the area that would become Wardensville, ten miles above Yellow Spring.

Historians disagree about the arrangements Washington worked out with the settlers. Although Samuel Kercheval refers to Fairfax's "insatiable disposition for the monopoly of wealth," his description of the baron's terms suggests that they were not onerous. "The lands were granted by Fairfax in fee simple to his tenants, subject to an annual rent of two shillings per hundred acres . . . added to which Fairfax required the payment of ten shillings sterling on each 50 acres (which he termed 'compensation money'), which was paid on issuing the grant." It was specified that the rental payments be made annually at Fairfax's Greenway Court "at the time of the feast of St. Michael the Archangel."

Morton identifies a shilling as being equivalent to twenty-five cents, so Fairfax's annual rental charge was fifty cents per hundred acres. There is no record of objection to the price. Most of the settlers were apparently anxious to firm up their entitlements; although Washington was operating as Fairfax's agent, the abstracts all read "Surveyed for . . . [the named settler]." The settlers received written grants signed by Fairfax about a year after the surveys were made, possibly when they showed up at Greenway Court. One of the original Warden grants has been preserved.

Washington's personal perspective on the operation, and something of life then along Lost River, emerge from a letter he wrote during his November 1749 trek to a "Richard" whose last name time has erased:

> I have not sleeped above three nights or Four in a bed but after walking a good deal all the day lay down before the fire upon a little Hay Straw Fodder or bearskin whichever is to be had with man wife and Children like a Parcel of Dogs or Catts and happy's he that gets the birth nearest the fire there's nothing would make it pass off tolerably but a good reward a Dubbleloon is my constant gain every day that the weather will permit my going out and sometimes Six Pistoles . . .

If Washington's syntax hadn't improved, he was doing well in applied arithmemtic. A doubloon, equivalent to two pistoles, was worth from thirty-six to forty shillings, or about six pounds, in Virginia currency. The surveyor had to cover his expenses out of this, including two shillings and six pence a day to his assistant. Washington's reported daily gain of 40 to 120 shillings compared favorably with the annual rental of two shillings per hundred acres which was to go from the settlers to Lord Fairfax. Most of the surveyor's compensation, though he was Fairfax's agent, apparently came from the land holders. The agent may well have profited more than his principal from the enterprise.

After completing the survey for William Warden, the

surveyor and his chainman, John Lonem, returned to Greenway Court. Caudy Davis's margin of error had been reduced to the ten miles that separate present-day Wardensville from Yellow Spring.

The story still isn't over.

After spending the winter in other occupation, Washington returned in the spring of 1750 to Greenway Court and came once more in Fairfax's service to the Great Cacapehon. John Lonem was again with him.

Working first in what is now the Capon Bridge area, the surveyor and his chainman then headed back up the valley to the Warden property, where they had left off in November. This means that on Sunday, April 1st, 1750, they rode across "our" land. But Mister Caudy's story was that Washington actually surveyed it.

On April 2nd, Washington and Lonem laid off three tracts on Trout Run, which enters the Capon at Wardensville, for Even Pugh, Jacob Pugh, and Joseph Powell; and another "on Cacapehon" for Thomas Hughs. On April 3rd they did two more along the river for Hugh Hughs and his son, William. There was another the next morning for William Hughs, Junr.

That same afternoon, Washington measured out a 400-acre tract for Nicholas Robinson. It included the present sites of the Yellow Spring mill, general store, garage, and post office. Caudy Davis was now one mile from vindication.

The next morning, Washington and Lonem veered off the course they had been following along the river, to measure a piece for William Welton. But by noon, they had turned back. The next abstract describes the tract they laid out for Edward Kinnison, Junr.—"Land on . . . Cacapehon."

The abstract that follows in G. Washington's field book, dated April 5th, differs from the others in one respect. The previous tracts had been laid off for resident settlers. This abstract starts, "Then surveyed for John Lonem. . . ." Washington's chainman, who had apparently come with him from eastern Virginia, must have taken a fancy to what was an unsettled tract. The abstract goes on:

> . . . a certain Tract of Waste Land Situate, Lying and being in Frederick County, and on Cacapehon and bounded as followeth beg: at two white Oaks under a clift of Rocks Edward Kinnison's Corner & run thence No. 37° Et Two hundd & forty Poles to two hickorys & white Oak on Mountain Side . . .

Coming to this abstract in the appendix to Toner's edition of Washington's journal, I turned to our 1967 title deed. The metes and bounds set out there read:

> Beginning at two white oak stumps, Kennison corner; thence No. 37 E . . .

Caudy Davis was exactly right. The two white oak stumps have now returned to the soil, but the "clift of Rocks" stands unchanged. It is pleasant to sit at my desk, look out the back window, and see, a hundred feet away, an eighteen-year-old boy walking along the base of the mountain on his way to becoming the father of his country.

The rest of the account, anticlimactic as far as Tannery's tale is concerned, rounds out the picture of the early settling of the Yellow Spring area. Washington and Lonem moved on down the river the next day to lay out plats for Darby McKeever and his son and one for Richard Arnold, Jun'r, later the site of Hook's Mill. Moving over to North River, a Cacapehon tributary, to pick up six squatters there, and then doubling back on April 16th to the Lost River area for several surveys (including one for a "William Miller Horse Jockey"), they returned to Fairfax's Greenway Court.

During the next two years, Washington carried on his surveying from an office he set up in the log building that is now a museum at the corner of South Braddock and West Cork streets in Winchester. Two other notebooks show that he returned to the Cacapehon several times—once to lay out a tract for Roger Parke (next to Darby McKeever), again to take care of Solomon Carpenter (adjoining Thomas Hughs) and Jeremiah Hook. The fact that he used John Lonem as his chainman whenever he was in this area suggests that, if it matters, Washington probably slept here at Tannery too.

Crosschecking with other records confirms the relative completeness, with one intriguing exception, of the Washington notebooks as a census of the Yellow Spring area, 1750. The Nicholas Robinson cabin was probably about where the mill is now, nestled like most of the others at the base of the mountain for warmth in the winter and coolness in the summer. The Weltons lived upriver, the Hughses and Carpenters above them, and the Woodfins a little to the east. Below on the river were the Kinnisons, John Lonem (apparently with his family), the McKeevers, and Jeremiah Hook. All of British descent, these early settlers had come south from Pennsylvania or New Jersey, probably following the wagon trail from the Potomac to Frederick Town and then probing another twenty-five miles west to satisfy their instinct or desire for independence or whatever it was that made them willing to assume isolation's high risks.

As far as I can determine, Washington's list omits only one of this area's original settlers. John Cale was probably the first to build a cabin here, a little down-river, near what would become Hooks Mill. This would have been in the early 1740s. The McKeevers apparently arrived three or four years later and were his neighbors. Yet Washington's records include no reference to Cale.

Trying to find a reason for this, I came to the realization that virtually all of the names in Washington's notebooks are of English, Irish, Scotch, or Welsh derivation. John Cale had come from Germany. I had wondered about the young surveyor's slighting reference in his journal to "as Ignorant a Set of People as the Indians they would never speak English but when spoken to they speak all Dutch." About to claim copyright on a novel interpretation of a tidbit of American history, I discovered that Winchester historian Oren Frederic Morton has a prior claim. He concludes that when Fairfax cut his deal with Joist Hite and James Wood, dividing up the disputed land rights, part of the arrangement with Hite, who had been born in Strasbourg, Alsace, was that his Lordship would not bother any squatters of German descent. Deutschland über alles.

Washington's role in history won't be diminished by the fact that in Caudy Davis's professional view he was only a mediocre surveyor. His equipment was elementary, a compass with a sighting glass attached, a Jacob's staff to rest it on, a sixteen-and-a-half-foot pole, and a chain that was stretched out to measure the line.

The compass was sufficiently accurate to identify degrees but not minutes, and after he and his chainman had laid out one side of a tract they frequently didn't bother to walk the other three, projecting them instead mathematically—so many poles along ninety-degree angles. Arguments still flare up along the Cacapon about Washington metes and bounds that have turned out to be off by feet or yards or even poles or rods.

When we bought our way into this scrap of history in 1967, Romney attorney Loudoun Thompson, representing the seller, asked us: "Do you want to do this your way or ours?" He pointed to the phrase in the deed that described the property (which is only part of John Lonem's original tract) as "160 acres more or less." "We'll do it your way," I agreed. "That's good," Loudoun replied, "because otherwise it would mean a whole new survey." His question was really whether what was good enough for George Washington was good enough for the Wirtzes. It was.

Appalachian Apartheid

Nicholas Robinson and his Capon Valley neighbors probably made it once, possibly twice, to Greenway Court on the feast day of St. Michael to lay their annual land rents on the altar of the Sixth Baron of Cameron. But they didn't pay their homage often. By 1753, the settlers were too busy at home with some other title claimants—long-time residents who had tolerated the intrusion of lighter-skinned aliens on ancient hunting grounds, until, repeatedly double-crossed, they raised the price of continued trespass to a lifted scalp, collectible on the spot. St. Michael, the militant and avenging archangel, probably understood and approved.

There is no clear record of human life in the valley before the European migration in the eighteenth century. The only artifacts are arrowheads and other flint specimens that turn up occasionally during the spring plowing in the fields along the river. An axehead seven inches long found several years ago at Camp Rim Rock, a quarter of a mile below Tannery, has been carbon dated by the Smithsonian Institution as fifteenth century or earlier. The Indian mound at Romney, twenty-five miles west, dates back to what paleontologists identify as the Woodland period—1,000 B.C.-1,000 A.D. No shards or other signs of early domestic establishment have been discovered along the Cacapon.

It isn't clear which Indian tribes were living here in the valley. Baden Larrick, leading local orchardist, says they were Shawnee and that their village was in Capon Hollow beside the spring, where the hotel is now. Baden probably knows, for in Larrick family tradition one of its immigrant members married a Shawnee and fathered fourteen children.

Historian Samuel Kercheval reports this as Catawba territory. He and Baden may both be right; the Shawnees and Catawbas were compatible and peaceful tribes. Various reports suggest that the Catawbas were "relatively advanced, intelligent and energetic," that they were more tolerant than the Iroquois and Algonquins of pale-skinned trespass on their hunting grounds, and that in the early eighteenth century they numbered at least eight thousand. The valley was also used as a hunting ground by the more militant Delawares, who came down frequently from the north.

In any event, whatever tribes were here joined in the anti-apartheid uprising that broke out after the colonists' breach of the 1753 Treaty of Logstown, which had drawn a line for white expansionism at the Ohio River. The same thing had happened earlier when the 1744 Treaty of Lancaster, with the Alleghenies set as the dividing line, was dishonored as soon as it was written, and before that when the Virginia authorities had promised the Iroquois in the 1732 Treaty of Albany not to settle west of the Blue Ridge.

The colonists knew what they were doing. On May 1, 1739 Quaker leader Thomas Chambley sent a letter to the monthly meeting of his flock at Opequon, a few miles northeast of what would become Yellow Spring:

> I desire you to be very careful, being far back inhabitants, to keep a friendly correspondence with the native Indians. . . . The Virginians have made an agreement with the natives to go as far as the [Blue Ridge] mountains and no farther, and you are over and beyond the mountains, therefore out of the agreement, by which you lie open to the insults and incursions of the . . . Indians.

When the 1753 Treaty was immediately and flagrantly violated, the tribes, egged on by French troops and military advisers who had come down from Canada with their own land-grabbing notions, decided to fight their way back to the line originally drawn at the Blue Ridge. Although the major encounters of the French and Indian War took place along the Ohio River and near the Great Lakes, the valley of the Great Cacapehon, twenty miles west of the Blue Ridge, became by the mid-1750s life-threatening territory.

Shamelessly rewritten in terms of bold white men and brave women risking martyrdom at the fiery stakes and the tomahawks of heathen savages standing in the way of Christianity's beneficent and ennobling advance, this history is a vivid and lurid chapter in valley folklore. One of its heroes is James Caudy, the "I. Coddy" in Washington's journal, with whom surveyor William Genn and his party had stayed overnight in 1748. His property included a spectacular bluff, still called Caudy's Castle, rising 500 feet almost straight up from the river several miles below Capon Bridge.

"Tradition relates," in historian Samuel Kercheval's favorite phrase, that when Caudy detected an Indian prowler following him he would pretend to flee along a trail that led up the back of the bluff. Near the top the path moved to the river side, becoming at one point a narrow rock shelf. Edging his way around the front of the bluff, the intrepid pioneer would step back into a recess in the rock, wait for his pursuer to come along, and then topple the hapless brave over the edge and down several hundred feet. Tradition doesn't explain the Indians' apparent willingness to play repeatedly at this game of redskin roulette, but Caudy reportedly carried it off so often that he is immortal locally as an Indian fighter.

The story of Darby McKeever's more typical defensive measures comes from Charles Anderson's encyclopedic and precise memory, one of the valley's treasure troves. Charles lives below Camp Rim Rock on the site where McKeever and his sons had their cabin. When the Indian hostility increased, they added on a second story that jutted out a little and had slits instead of windows in the walls. When an attack came, the family went upstairs and the men fired down on the marauding Indians. Holes in the second-story floor permitted the McKeevers to pour water, kept in two barrels, on any fires set by Indians below.

Another familiar account is of the fate of Susan Day, who lived with her husband Nathaniel and their family "in the Cacapon River neighborhood, near Capon Springs," four miles south of Yellow Spring. Kercheval reports that "at about the time of Braddock's defeat," which was in 1755, Susan and her ten-year-old daughter Martha were kidnapped by a party of Indians, probably Delawares, and taken off into the hills. Susan, the story goes, was required to take off her shoes, from which she concluded (by a logic Kercheval doesn't explain) that she was going to be killed, which she told Martha. Tearing off little pieces of her skirt, Susan dropped them along the path as signs for a rescue party to follow.

Susan's premonition proved right and her artifice partially effective. She was scalped that night "on a mountain between Cacapon River and Cedar Creek." But a party of twenty men, led by a Captain Frye and including Martha's brother John, was already on the petticoat trail. Catching up with the Indians early the next morning, Captain Frye's posse shot one of them. The others fled, leaving Martha, unharmed, behind.

Jane and I have a special interest in the Day story. One of the certifiable descendants of Susan and Nathaniel Day was Dr. James A. Day, a family physician in Jacksonville, Illinois, who presided on February 28, 1913 at the entry onto the human scene of one Mary Jane Quisenberry, who later assumed the alias Jane Wirtz and is currently Tannery's presiding mistress. Dr. Day's son Edward and his wife Mary Louise are among our closest lifetime friends. Ed has filled in from his own family research the additional information—which Kercheval missed—that the Martha Day who escaped from the Indians later married John Kinnison and lived for a time right next door to where we do now. The Days have given us almost personal legitimacy in valley history and legend.

Despite the Caudy and McKeever and Day brands of resourcefulness the Yellow Spring area finally had to be abandoned by the settlers. Some of them took refuge in a small fort hastily constructed on the Edwards property at what is now Capon Bridge. Others made their way to larger Fort Loudoun at Winchester (on the hill just north of where Loudoun and Piccadily streets intersect today), which Virginia's Governor Robert Dinwiddie put under the command, in 1755, of a newly commissioned lieutenant colonel of the Virginia Regiment, twenty-three-year-old George Washington.

In an April 24, 1756 letter to the Virginia Assembly, Washington reported that "North Mountain [the eastern shoulder of the Lost River and Capon valleys] . . . is now become our exterior bound, there not being one inhabitant beyond that (to the west) . . . except a few families on the South Branch, and at Joseph Edward's on the Cacapon . . . guarded by a party of ours." A year later, Captain John Mercer and thirty of his men were massacred when they marched into an Indian ambuscade outside Fort Edwards.

After two or three years of constant tension, the Indians, badly outnumbered, began withdrawing to the west and the bolder settlers returned to the valley. Some of them too soon. One of the McKeevers was killed and scalped when he went out from his blockhouse cabin to hunt on the mountain. William Warden was done in by a band of Delawares along Lost River in 1758.

But there were fewer natives than trespassers, and by 1765 the hostilities were declared over. King George III's Royal Proclamation of 1763 had purported to reestablish the Appalachians as the westward boundary of British settlement, but during the next few years the colonial governments made, then broke, treaties with various Indian nations. "The Indian tribes" were written into the American Constitution, and in 1790 one of the first President's initial acts was to sign personally, with leaders of the Indian nations, the Treaty of New York. It, too, went up in smoke at the Battle of Fallen Timbers in 1794. The frustrated Indians turned to fighting each other, and those who survived were driven onto reservations or across the Mississippi.

So what I see as I look out the back window through history's perspective gets murkier than it was at first. The eighteen-year-old boy, agent of a titled British immigrant, walks his line with a Jacob's staff over his shoulder, North 37 degrees East, into memorable American tradition. But another figure comes into view. A young Indian hunter, son of the sons of generations like him, looking up the mountainside for small game or deer, walks along the same line . . . into extinction. The two images blur into an indelible stain on American history.

The ten years of tree-to-tree fighting and cabin burning resulted in a substantial turnover of the original tiny Yellow Spring population. The title line that came down from Nicholas Robinson, original owner of Yellow Spring proper, has been lost, but at some point in the 1760s or 1770s his holdings passed into the hands of the Klein family. Henry Frye from the Wardensville area purchased the Hughs, Woodfin, and probably Welton, acreage in a series of transactions recorded in the 1750s.

John Lonem, our own titular ancestor in possession, lived here only briefly. It was long enough that the little stream that crosses our property on the other side of the river is still called Loman's Branch, the name having been altered only slightly by local standards. A good many of the Fairfax records survived the burning of Richmond and are now in the Virginia State

Library there. Page 270 of Northern Neck Grant Book K carries the report that Lonem assigned his property on March 20, 1761 to a Samuel Pritchard, and that two weeks later, on April 7, Pritchard transferred it to one Moses Watkins. Lonem disappeared from history's view, and as far as can be told Watkins never assumed actual occupancy. The tract appears to have gone unused until John Parrill took it over late in the century.

The Kinnisons, our neighbors two centuries removed, were among those who spent some of the war months as Colonel Washington's beleaguered guests at Fort Loudoun in Winchester. The colonel's meticulous records list several small payments to "Kate Kinnison, nurse, at the hospital." Returning only briefly to the valley, the Kinnisons and their in-laws, the Days, moved off to stake out new claims farther back in the mountains. Most of the Kinnison property shows up in the records a few years later in the possession of the Cump family.

By 1775 or so, this was still a deep backwoods area unconnected with anyplace. A dozen families, some newly arrived, lived in isolated cabins along an eight-mile stretch of river. Their driving desire was to be left alone. Veterans of a war they had invited, the last thing they wanted was another . . . a revolution for independence, which was one thing they felt they already had.

Of Revolution and Roots

On a Saturday afternoon in July of 1986, a hundred or so people gathered at the Old Kump Graveyard, in a field corner across the river from Tannery, to dedicate a memorial stone bearing the name of Henry Cump, who served in the Revolutionary War, and his wife Juliah. Although it hadn't rained for a month, the sky darkened a few minutes before the ceremony was to start, and just as the representatives of the South Branch Daughters of the American Revolution took their places and the Wardensville Veterans of Foreign Wars Color Guard presented the colors there was a deluge. Thunder roared and lightning flashed. The gathering broke ranks and dispersed.

I had two errant thoughts as Jane and I ran for our car. One seemed worth shouting to the color guardsman beside me. "Very appropriate," I called out. "A twenty-one-gun salute direct from headquarters." He either didn't hear or counted the remark treasonably beneath notice.

The other reaction came from some research I had done into Yellow Spring's part in the Revolution. The area's contribution was meager. Henry Cump's service was modest, and one other local resident, John Cale, made an even less historic effort. Everybody else stayed home. A mystic might have found in the celestial cancellation of the dedication service some war god's outpouring of two centuries of pent-up exasperation with the ambivalent patriotism that emerged along the Cacapon in 1776.

In fairer judgment, the valley settlers' sentiments about the Revolution are easily understood. Living deep in a wilderness, hard pressed with the day-to-day demands of keeping families alive, they felt little concern about excise taxes on tea coming into Boston Harbor or about British impressment of colonial sailors on the high seas. Those pioneers who "spoke all Dutch" when a young surveyor approached them a few years earlier, couldn't react strongly to Thomas Paine's pamphlets. Others with British names had passed too quickly through seaboard ports of entry to become imbued with colonial resentments. "Taxation without representation" was a poor rallying cry in this remote valley that was untouched by the one and uninterested in the other.

An incident that occurred late in the war reflects this underdeveloped sense of patriotism. The Virginia legislature had made its eighth call on the various counties of the state for additional troops; Hampshire's quota this time was sixty-three men, "each soldier to be not less than five feet four inches, not a deserter or subject to fits, but . . . able-bodied and of sound mind and fit for immediate service."

At Petersburg, near the headwaters of Lost River,

the response to this call was an assembly of some fifty men under the leadership of citizens John Claypole and John Brake. They voted not to pay taxes to the state, then drank a toast "to the health of George the III and damnation to Congress," and refused to enlist in the colonial cause. When General Daniel Morgan, in charge of the revolutionary forces at Winchester, heard of the uprising, he marched 400 militia to Petersburg, routed out the insurgents, killed several of them, and took Claypole and Brake to Romney. Imprisoned and convicted by the Court of Oyer and Terminer, they were later pardoned by the governor of Virginia.

Historians report that Hampshire County met the legislature's successive calls on it and that its citizens served with distinction throughout the Revolutionary War. Yet even strong civic pride in Cacapon and Lost River history doesn't erase the suspicion that the general sentiment in these valleys was spoken by Claypole and Brake at Petersburg.

Looking into the record of Yellow Spring's revolutionary connection reveals another story that is more meaningful than a traditional account of local military heroism. It is an account of roots instead of revolution, of bloodlines rather than battles.

In addition to Henry Cump's and John Cale's service, two other veterans of the fighting moved to Yellow Spring after it was over. So did the daughter of another credentialed warrior. This still doesn't add up to very many patriots. Surprisingly, however, most of Yellow Spring's authentic residents today qualify for membership in the Daughters of the American Revolution, or its male auxiliary.

So it seems worthwhile to trace briefly the family

lines of Henry Cump and John Cale, and the three new settlers—George Nicholas Spaht, Philip Klein, and Jane McKee LaFollette—to get a sense of the variety of roots that Yellow Spring grew from and how these roots wove together and survived.

The part of this story that has been memorialized in the monument across the river goes back to 1772 when a George Cump moved to the valley with his wife and took, by a grant from Lord Fairfax, part of what had earlier been the Kinnison tract. The young couple had migrated from Germany to Bucks County, Pennsylvania, in the 1750s. Their children had been born there, son Henry in 1757.

When a certain George Sly ("of Hampshire County") was drafted for military service in May of 1781, he arranged for young Henry Cump, then twenty-four, to substitute for him. War Department Pension Records identify Cump's service as "under Captain Stump in the Army of General Anthony Wayne." Following this tour of duty, Henry was himself drafted in October of 1781 for three months' service "under Captain Parsons, guarding prisoners in Winchester," and then stayed on at the prison camp for several months more, under Captain James Eaton, as a substitute for Daniel Loy.

Although the Cump lineage hasn't been fully unraveled, Henry and two brothers passed on the name, eventually changed to Kump, to Yellow Spring's most widely known family. The Kump landholdings extended up Loman's Branch, and included the property on which the Brills had built the red brick house that is a Yellow Spring landmark today—the Kump, more recently the Aikin, place.

The Kump family's ascendancy in local and state history came through two brothers, Garnett Kerr (born in 1875) and Herman Guy (1877), sons of Benjamin Franklin III and Margaret Francis Randolph Kump. After being educated at the local Mt. Airy School and at the University of West Virginia, the brothers went on to successful law practices and distinguished public service careers. Garnett became a member of the West Virginia House of Delegates (1905-1907), the state Senate (1912-1920), and the Twenty-Second Judicial Circuit Court (1928-1936). Younger brother Herman went even further. After service as captain in the U.S. Army Ordinance, stationed in Washington during World War I, he too became a Circuit Court Judge (Twentieth District, 1928-1932), and was then elected governor of West Virginia (1933-1937).

John Cale, Yellow Spring's other enlistee, was the early settler George Washington had overlooked, by either inadvertence or design, in his 1750 survey. Born on April 4, 1726, of German ancestry, John had come to the valley as a very young man in about 1745, taking up a considerable tract of land on the west side of the river, immediately below what Washington later laid out as the McKeever property. On July 25, 1751, John married Elizabeth Pugh, a member of the Even or Jacob Pugh family who had done business with surveyor Washington the year before upriver in the Trout Run area.

John Cale's war record is curious. Although the DAR records are clear and confident, they offer no clue to what prompted Yellow Spring's earliest settler to decide, when he was fifty years old, to join up as a private in the Eighth Virginia Regiment under the command of Colonel Abraham Bowman and Captain William Croghan. This was several months before war was declared. He remained in the service only "from 1st day of March to last of April." (My personal suspicion that the sixty-day patriot was a son, John Cale, Jr. would belie the DAR and other records.)

The Cales had another ironic connection with the War for Independence. In 1781, a young man named George Nicholas Spaht began courting their daughter Elizabeth. Although he, too, was a veteran of the recently ended fighting, Spaht had marched to a different drumbeat.

George's story, a footnote to familiar Revolutionary history, involved the German Duke Ferdinand of Hesse. Short of funds and devoid of principle, the duke made a business of selling off his young male subjects to King George III of England to serve against the uprising in his Majesty's American colonies. One of the chattels in this low-overhead enterprise was a sixteen-year-old boy who was abducted by the duke's agents as he was walking to school in Kassel, the capital of Hesse. Packed off to a seaport and shipped COD to America, young George Nicholas Spaht was soon carrying a musket he hardly knew how to handle, caring even less about using it.

Lacking taste for their involuntary labors, the Hessians turned out to be poor soldiers, prone to improve the earliest opportunity for surrender. Special prison camps were set up for them, one at Winchester. George Nicholas Spaht, captured by Washington's troops at Trenton, New Jersey, took up involuntary residence at Winchester in late 1776 or early 1777.

When the war ended, young Spaht found his way to the Capon Valley, and in 1782 married Elizabeth Cale. Some place along the line, George decided to call a Spaht a Spaid, and his bride's family changed their Cale to Kale.

Taking land near the Kale property, the 120-acre tract that surveyor Washington had laid out for Roger Park in 1752, the young couple proceeded to atone actively for any offense King George's involuntary hireling might have done the new nation. Albert Thompson Secrest accounts in his 1922 *Spaid Genealogy* for their nine children, sixty-eight grandchildren, and 383 great-grandchildren. In her two-volume classic, *The Capon Valley: It's Pioneers and Their Descendants* (the spelling is the author's), Maud Pugh notes of George Nicholas Spaht that "Capon Valley is indebted to him for early teaching service" and remarks that "on Capon the Spaid connection includes members of nearly every family from Hooks Mill to Intermont and Capon Springs." In 1821, George and Elizabeth signed their property over to Benjamin Cackley and moved to Ohio. The family may have gotten to be too much for them.

Veteran Philip Klein was also of German descent, the son of immigrants John Jacob and Eva Dusong Klein, who arrived in this country on October 17, 1749 aboard the vessel *Fane,* captained by William Hyndman. Landing at Philadelphia, John and Eva signed, as they were required to, an oath that attested their fealty to the King of England—but included no commitment covering such progeny as they might produce.

The family moved in 1764 to Stephensburg, twenty-five miles east of Yellow Spring, and with the outbreak of war their young son Philip, age seventeen, went back to Pennsylvania and enlisted in the German Regiment. Serving in Captain David Woelpper's company, he was wounded at the Battle of Germantown in 1777, "bloody year of the three sevens," but returned when he recovered to become a member of Captain George Ball's company in Frederick County, Virginia. He took part in the siege of Yorktown that ended with Cornwallis's surrender in 1781.

During the war, John and Eva Klein had moved to Yellow Spring, taking up a substantial tract of land on the river, next to the Cumps, on part of what had been Kinnison and Robinson property. Joining his parents after the war was over, Philip married Elizabeth Schweitzer, daughter of Johannes and Anna Maria (Hawk) Schweitzer, at the new Lutheran Church on March 31, 1791. The ceremony was performed by Reverend Christian Streit, who had been Philip's chaplain during the war and had then come to the Yellow Spring area.

Philip and Elizabeth established, through their fourteen sons and daughters, another broad base of Yellow Spring family history. Two of their grandsons, Asa (Asie) and Lemuel (Lem), served in the Confederate forces during the Civil War, fathered large families, and at one time owned quite a bit of land along the river. Lemuel, who had the brick house that is now the church retreat directly across the river from Tannery, was the grandfather of our neighbor John Kline, the community's cherished citizen until his death in 1984.

One of history's smaller ironies, suggesting how little is ever new in the annals of fumbling government bureaucracy, emerges from the pension records for Henry Cump and Philip Klein. When Henry, whose service had been undistinguished, died in 1849, it was neighbor and compatriot Philip who arranged for Henry's widow Juliah to get his veteran's pension. But when Philip, battle-scarred veteran of several campaigns, died four years later, his widow Elizabeth was denied a pension. Professing difficulty in sorting out the

Kleins, Klines, and Clines, the Commissioner of Pensions in Washington also rejected a detailed affidavit sworn to by Philip's younger brother, Anthony; the affiant would have been, the commissioner divined, only three years old in 1780 (a critical date) "and couldn't possibly remember as much as he has sworn to." A much later petition to the higher court of the DAR was more successful; though worthless to Elizabeth, it resulted in Philip Klein's name being duly inscribed on page 392 of Volume I of the Patriot Index in the DAR library in Washington.

The valley's claim on Revolutionary War veteran Robert McKee, who served as a colonel in the Second Virginia Militia, is marginal, for after the war he settled several miles east, on the far end of Timber Ridge. But in 1795, on New Year's Day, the colonel's daughter, Jane, married one William LaFollette. They moved to Yellow Spring—to raise ten children and become, along with the Kumps, Kales, Spaids, and Klines, the area's genealogically distinguished progenitors.

When Jane and I first met the local LaFollettes, we wondered whether they were related to the Wisconsin branch which played so large a part in American politics during the 1930s, when we were college students in Beloit, Wisconsin. The two lines do in fact diverge from a common ancestor, two centuries ago.

As far as recorded history tells, that story starts with Jean DuFollet, a Huguenot living in Anjou Province in France during the eighteenth century when Catholics confiscated property as the price of Protestant fidelity. Considerable evidence bolsters the legend that Jean sacrificed his business as a silk merchant, spirited his fiancee from the convent in which her less committed Huguenot parents had stored her, and fled to the Isle of Jersey. The DuFollets migrated to the colony of New Jersey, joining a settlement of other Huguenots established near Newark.

This odyssey took an unhappy turn during the Colonial War, in the late 1750s, when French invaders from Canada, of Catholic faith, instigated an Indian attack on the Huguenot settlement in New Jersey. A Jean DuFollet, either the original Protestant or a son of the same name, was burned at the stake. His three boys, Joseph, Charles, and Georges, escaped by virtue of the good fortune that had sent them that day to the country to have some corn ground at a water mill.

By one account, the three brothers all served in the Revolutionary War under the Marquis de Lafayette, their fellow Frenchman who had come to America to assist the colonial cause. According to this version, when the three brothers were mustered out of the army at Norfolk, Virginia in 1783, they changed their family name to LaFollette out of respect for the redoubtable marquis.

More careful research confirms military service by only one of the brothers—Joseph—who fought for three years with Pulaski's Foreign Legion, served as head wagoneer in Washington's commissariat, and was wounded while serving under Lafayette's command at Brandywine in 1777. Joseph was the ancestor of Robert Marion ("Fighting Bob") LaFollette, governor of Wisconsin, congressman and senator, and the Progressive Party's unsuccessful candidate for the presidency in 1924.

Brother Georges LaFollette (not recognized as a Revolutionary War veteran by the DAR) and his wife Jemima Hawthorne came to the Capon Valley in the mid to late 1770s. Making their first home near the Cales, they built a log cabin over on Back Creek, "when Jefferson was Governor" according to family tradition (which would make it between 1779 and 1781).

It was their son William who took as his bride in 1795 Jane McKee, the Revolutionary colonel's daughter. Their ten children would marry into the Brill, Spaid, Pennington, Capper, and Anderson families. Descendant Margaret Spaid LaFollette, now in her nineties, lives in the home place on Back Creek, next door to her son Russell and his wife Ruby, whose orchids and begonias and cacti appear in most Yellow Spring homes and yards and whose marigolds and tomatoes thrive in our garden.

This point and counterpoint of early military and later family history seems to mock a little American genealogy's preoccupation with Revolutionary credentials. So few did so much for so many descendants by virtue of relatively slight front-line activity. The close family linkage remains, though, a critical element in the Yellow Spring character. Four of these names—Spaid, Kump, Kline, LaFollette—are as common in the valley today as they were two centuries ago. Yellow Spring has become (with careful attention to the no-closer-than-second-cousin-injunction) a seventh-generation extended family.

In the beginning that family had two distinct branches. Whatever prejudice prompted Washington to confine his surveying to settlers of British descent and to give the back of his journalistic hand to those who spoke "all Dutch" was reflected in the clear division within the early Yellow Spring settlement. The first wave of immigrants was predominantly, though not exclusively, of English, Scotch, Irish or Welsh descent. Among the British emigres, the McKeever, Pugh, Parks, Hook, Hughs, and Woodfin families, listed as landholders in 1750, returned to the valley after the French and Indian War. Jeremiah Reid and his family took up a 300-acre tract on the Ridge in 1777, and the Anderson, Racy, and Hannon families settled in the area by 1780.

During the period between the two wars the balance began to shift to a preponderance of German, Dutch, and Swiss immigrants. They brought the family names, subject to frequent change because only some of the settlers could write, that have become Fry (Frye), Swisher (Switzer, Schweitzer, Schweitzerin), Hawk (Hack, Haak, Haack, Hackin), Baumgardner, Loy, Huber (Huberin), Rudolph, Hotsinpillar (with variations too numerous to mention), and others.

Henry Frye, born in Germany in 1724, was part of this contingent. Settling first in the Wardensville area in the 1750s, he later moved downriver to Intermont, and bought up a considerable acreage along the Capon.

The three Schweitzer brothers—Johannes, Valentine, and Nicholas—were of German or Swiss descent. Arriving in Philadelphia on September 17, 1753, aboard the *Patience* out of Rotterdam, they came to the Capon Valley soon after that, settling near Intermont.

The earliest settler in the area back up the hollow that is now Capon Springs was probably Peter Hotsinpillar, son or grandson of the German-born Stephen Hotsinpillar who arrived in Philadelphia in 1728 aboard the *Mortonhouse*. In 1793, Peter's daughter Christine was married at the Lutheran Church at Intermont to George Rudolph, Jr., whose family had come from Württemberg, Germany to Shenandoah County,

Virginia sometime before 1780. They purchased a 400-acre tract on the river at Intermont in 1808.

A third immigrant strain in the valley was essentially French Huguenot. It included the LaFollettes and the Brills. Johann Herman Brill came with his wife (of whom, typically, nothing was recorded or is remembered) to the Star Tannery area in Frederick County, Virginia some time before 1790. He was one of three brothers who had been members of a distinguished French family (originally spelled de Briel or de Breil) of armigerous rank in Normandy, which entitled them to have a coat of arms. They had fled from religious persecution to the Palatinate in Germany and then had come to this country in 1754.

Johann Brill's son, Henry Jefferson, married Elizabeth Orndorff, of Star Tannery, Virginia, and in the late 1790s, according to family records, they "crossed the [North] mountain on foot, carrying a large iron kettle." They built a log cabin on "Lomond's Branch," where they raised six sons and three daughters. Their great-great-granddaughter, Willetta, is our close friend and neighbor, Forrest Davis's wife.

I started to indulge my professional curiosity about the land transactions that were incident to these arrivals in the area. Where did the newcomers get their titles? And what happened to Lord Thomas Fairfax's claims to proprietorship of this whole "Northern Neck"?

Only a little of the story seemed in the end worth pursuing. After the hostilities with the French and Indians were over, some of the settlers took up their annual treks to Greenway Court to pay their two shillings per hundred acres to Fairfax. Others, perhaps considering his lordship's term unreasonable, gave up their claims, which were then transferred to new owners. Fairfax's entitlement ended completely after the Revolutionary War when the Virginia legislature formally confiscated all titles that had imperial roots, specifically providing that "the landholders within the said district of the Northern Neck shall be forever hereafter exonerated and discharged from composition and quitrent, any law, custom or usage, to the contrary notwithstanding."

Jilted again, this time by history, in what had been his second love affair, Fairfax accepted the verdict with dignity, grace, and resignation. A steadfast Loyalist, he stayed out of the revolutionary struggle, perhaps watching with mixed feelings as the boy next door, whom he had helped make, presided at the creation of a new nation that rejected all concepts of a titled nobility. Fairfax remained in quiet residence at Greenway Court, never permitting a woman to cross its threshold except for domestic service. Using part of his still ample means to develop a magnificent personal library, he also contributed substantial funds to the episcopacy in Winchester. Dying a few months after the 1781 Cornwallis surrender at Yorktown, Lord Fairfax was buried beneath the floor of the church.

By the end of the century the Yellow Spring area included within its four-mile radius thirty or forty families, many of them large and counting rapidly, a total population of several hundred. These families remained widely scattered, prisoners of distance and remoteness. The men drove hogs for several days to Winchester, to exchange them for a year's supply of salt, but this nearest town was too far away to get a sick child or a crushed leg there in time to do any good.

The humbling lesson that emerges in history's perspective is of the human capacity to play solitaire against untamed nature's awesome odds.

Historian-genealogist Maud Pugh writes with aptly plain eloquence of her eighteenth-century Capon Valley ancestors:

> Cut off . . . by lack of roads and transportation . . . they set about making provision for their . . . needs by building mills, tanneries, . . . ferries, forts, etc. The flax hackler, the distaff, the spinning wheel, the hand looms, the swift flying needle, the pressboard, and goose irons were necessary adjuncts. They grew their own flax and wool and manufactured it in the home, used wild fruits and pounded the corn in a mortar at first, dipped their own candles and burned pine knots, which were plentiful, in the wide, open fireplaces which they constructed from natural stones. . . . Without matches they struck a spark with flint into flax lint, or borrowed fire, if a neighbor lived close enough. They used honey from a bee tree to preserve the wild fruits and made sugar from sugar maple sap, grew tobacco which they cured and used as money, made their own brooms and utensils; had their own forge for blacksmithing where they made most of their farming tools and even nails for the erection of log houses. These logs were chiefly hearts of virgin pine, hand hewn with a broad-axe. Rafters of poles covered with oak shingles, hand riven and planed, or clapboards formed the roof.

Another family genealogist, Robert Reid, summarizes what he found in looking deeply into the lives of his early forebears who settled on Timber Ridge:

> Over and over our ancestors inherited and re-inherited a liking for the frontier. Historical and legal records establish that they are not to be classed as saints. Risk-

ing their scalps for a chance to better the lives of their descendants, they cannot be classified as softies. Like most pioneers, our ancestors were perhaps overinclined to take a chance on a 'win a horse or lose the saddle' basis. To their credit it can be said that after losing the saddle and their shirt along with it, they never 'walked back home to live with the wife's people.'

Faith Of Our Fathers

On the Eighteenth Sunday after Trinity, September 28, 1986, Pastors Phillip Huber and Samuel Scheiderer rode up to the Hebron Lutheran Church on horseback. Jack Rudolph, the president of the congregation, and his wife Ruth followed in a two-horsepower coach. The pastors, the Rudolphs, and many of the communicants gathered in front of the church were dressed in colonial apparel, ranging from frilled finery to an old pistol Jake Rudolph had stuck in his belt. It was the 200th anniversary of the first meeting of a "united German congregation on the 'Keb Kebron' "

Although the bicentennial date, like the costumery, was only approximate, and the pastors were uneasy in their saddles, the occasion was authentically historical. The anniversary was not just of the Lutheran Church at Intermont, three miles above Yellow Spring, but of two centuries of religion's dominant influence in shaping this community's character.

It is hard to grasp the place that religion had in the

valley's early history and the sustaining power it provided. Many of the settlers were refugees from religious controversy, so devout in their particular beliefs that they had chosen exile rather than compromise. They had left forms of worship set in vaulted and domed cathedrals and marked by pageants, oratorios and requiems, all kinds of religious pomp and circumstance. In sharp contrast, the faith they relied on in the wilderness was plain, simple, quiet, homespun like everything else in their new lives. They relied on prayer to carry them through torment and need and often tragic loss, constant fare in the valley's remoteness. Religion also gave them their only sense of community.

The clearest picture I can find of this is in a diary kept during the early nineteenth century by the Reverend William H. Foote, a Presbyterian missionary based in Romney who rode over the mountains to the Capon Valley. One lengthy entry, dated November 16, 1819, written after Foote's return from one of those visits, includes the earliest discovered description of the valley and the way people lived here:

> The morning was lowery, threatening rain, and the clouds riding low gave to the Capon mountains . . . a sable hue. They had always a dreary appearance, but now looked melancholy, as if draped in mourning. . . . Few houses were to be seen from the road, which is seldom passed by wagons. . . .
>
> I had proceeded not far before I met an old man riding a small black horse, his gray hairs from his bent shoulders hanging near his saddle-bow. I had approached near before he saw me. His bridle and saddle were like his raiment, relics of a past age. A hat in keeping with his costume crowned his head, which was bent near to his saddle. . . .
>
> As he answered my inquiry, "Is this the way to N--

------ L-----------? I am a missionary going there to preach," I told him my name and by whom sent.

"Sent by Wilson" said he, holding out his hand. "Welcome! I am N------- L-------. It is now a long time since missionaries came here. They used to come. There were Hill, and Glass, and Lyle; but none has been here for years. When do you want to preach? Have you no appointment?"

"None; I sent you one for tonight."

"Well, I never heard of it, but I will send word out now; it is not noon yet."

So he turned and led me along a narrow, winding path . . . Then suddenly turning we were on the brow of a steep precipice of no ordinary height. At our feet lay a beautiful scene. The Capon, running with fine stream, was in full view, making a semi-circular bend of more than a mile, the land within the bend level and in beautiful cultivation, little plots of plowed land, of grass, or orchards scattered over it, a few buildings, and near to us a little mill. . . . At our feet the Capon, at our left a continuation of the precipice on which we stood, beyond the little plot of land a high ridge of rocky mountains, and as far as the eye could reach all round tops of ridges, wild and fierce, and dark as the clouds that lowered about them. . . .

The house was small, one room sufficed for eating and cooking and working. The spinning wheels were laid aside, and the cooking commenced. . . . The chimney had its supply of choice sticks of various timber taking the smoke, drying for use.

"Go, son," said he to a stout young lad, "go, son, and tell neighbor -------, and tell him to tell his neighbor there will be preaching here, and go by neighbor ------- and tell him the same, and if you see anyone tell him the same, and I will give notice at the mill."

Towards middle of the afternoon I looked out and saw persons coming in different directions down the

mountains. I had seen so few places of residence that
I could not contrive whence they come. . . . I preached
from the words, "fear not, little flock, for it is your
Father's good pleasure to give you the kingdom."

After the congregation had dispersed I found that the
old man had fulfilled in part his duty as an elder in the
church by assembling his neighbors and reading to
them and praying with them, some few of whom are
religious. "My father and grandfather," said he, "were
pious. My grandfather came here and chose this spot
in preference to any of the Valley of Virginia, because
he thought it more healthy. There he was driven away
by the Indians—here my father lived. They taught me
my duty. They were French Protestants."

The Reverend Foote's visit in 1819 followed many
years of earlier missions that brought virtually every
faith that had been established in England and Europe
to the valley. Except for Catholicism. Many early settlers were descendants of victims of overreaching by
the Church of Rome. Yet even among those who shared
a history of protest, a jealous sectarianism sometimes
separated as many neighbors as it drew together. Circuit riders following close in the pioneers' wagon tracks
preached conflicting gospels, often warning as much
against the ecclesiastical competition as against the
devil.

The spreading of various faiths across the frontier
depended less on the missionaries' vigor than on what
creed various groups of settlers had brought with them.
Historian Samuel Kercheval relates that a Baptist
preacher named Stearns came from New England in
1754 and "settled for a short time on the Capon
River . . . but soon removed to North Carolina"; he apparently found too few adherents here. Despite Reverend Foote's eloquence and the early development of

a strong presbytery at Romney, he seems not to have found many along the Cacapon who shared N------- L------'s acceptance of rugged Calvinism and the tenet of predestination.

Quakers coming down from William Penn's colony not far to the north were probably the first missionaries to arrive in the area; there are records of a meeting at Opequon, twenty-five miles east of Yellow Spring, as early as 1730 or 1732. But the Friends, although widely admired, suffered a serious setback when their pacificism led to a number of them being jailed as traitors in the Revolutionary War prison camp at Winchester.

Robert Reid's genealogy of the Cowgill and George families, who settled along Back Creek and up on the ridge about 1780, includes a sensitive description of how their neighbors viewed the Friends:

> Most non-Quakers regarded Quakers as queer stubborn people. These same Americans had extremely high regard for a Quaker's honesty and truthfulness. If a Quaker said the horse he offered for sale was eight years old, the horse was. After failing to reach the Quakers with a heavy bribe, Oliver Cromwell said: 'This religion is the only one I ever met that could resist the Charms of Gold." Quakers were more than a hundred years ahead of the crowd as regards slavery and women's rights. Women were equal with men in all decisions at the meeting. Women and men were both registered as ministers of the Gospel.

The valley would have seemed a natural frontier for Episcopalian (Church of England) missionary efforts. Local landlord Thomas Fairfax came from a family that had been prominent in the revolt of the English Church against Catholicism, and Lord Fairfax's only apparent devotion, except money, was religion. Another of Winchester's founders, James Wood, was an Episcopalian vestryman. Predictably, the early settlers established in 1753 a new Church of England outpost at Romney. Maud Pugh, who describes her pioneer ancestors as "Church of England people," reports an Episcopalian preacher "holding early meetings on Capon drains," apparently near North River.

The Episcopalian mission aborted, however, with the outcome of the political revolution. The American Declaration of Independence was against a monarchy that asserted divine right and considered the kingdom and the Church of England inseparable. Of three Episcopalian clergymen ordained in 1771 "for Hampshire County" only one, "Reverend Mr. Manning," ever arrived; and when he was unable to muster enough support for a church in Romney he returned to England. At the close of the Revolution, Episcopal Bishop Lowth refused to ordain additional preachers to minister to the wayward American colonists.

Only three of the thousand pages in Bishop William Meade's compendious 1857 history of the episcopacy in Virginia (*Old Churches, Ministers and Families of Virginia*) are devoted to the Hampshire County parish, and his benediction on the early Episcopal experience here is tinged with failure's bitterness. "There are some winds against which even the power of steam proved ineffectual, and there are some places and societies where the excellences of our Church system and service cannot avail against violent and long established prejudices ... Such was the case in relation to this part of Virginia."

Strangely, there has never been a church at the center of the Yellow Spring area. The three faiths that grew the deepest roots—Lutheranism, Methodism, and the beliefs that were merged in the Christian Church—were held by handfuls of families living two or three miles away, at Intermont or Shiloh or back on Timber Ridge Road. These settlers built their log churches close to their homes.

Three Schweitzer families, who settled a little way upriver, near where Mutton Run comes down to enter the Capon, were particularly active in bringing together the German immigrants who arrived here in large numbers in the 1760s and 1770s. When Pastor Christian Streit, a Lutheran chaplain during the Revolutionary War, arrived in the early 1780s, he first held services in various homes and whenever circumstances permitted. Eventually the impetus developed for putting up the log church, two hundred years ago, at Intermont.

In their homeland, some of these newly arrived German families had been members of the Lutheran Synod, while others were from the reformed German branch of the church. Although this presented difficulties that loomed larger then than they would today, good sense prevailed and the United German Congregation was established. The new log structure was referred to as the Great Capon Church. An understanding was reached that membership on the church board would be divided equally and that pastors would be chosen in alternate years from the two branches. Lutheran Pastor Abraham C. Deshler from the Synod served the first year, succeeded by Reformed German Pastor John Lotroizer the next.

The list of communicants at the first service of the United German Congregation in November of 1786 includes seventeen names: four Schweitzers, three Hawks

(Hack, Hachlin), four Baumgartners, a Schumaker, a Wolf, a Perrill (or possibly Perzel), two Michels (Micklins), and John Huber, who was named trustee by the Reformed contingent. The services were in German and the church records were kept in that language until 1820. They include other names that are still familiar: Frye (Fry), Frankhauser (Funkhauser), LaFollette, Brill, Pennington, Rudolph, Strosnider.

These records testify eloquently to the deeply religious feelings of the early settlers. Ruth Ryan Rudolph, a present-day pillar of the church and its historian, puts this with characteristic sensitivity: "It is evident that, in spite of the difficulties involved in settling a new country, these pioneers believed that 'righteousness exalteth a nation' and that the church was just as essential to the real growth of the community as the houses, barns, fences and roads upon which they labored six days a week."

The Lutheran Church at Intermont is recognized as the oldest congregation, in terms of continual services, west of the Blue Ridge. The brick building erected in the 1840s to replace the original log structure stands as a monument to religion as the strongest and most sustaining force in valley history.

Being born a Methodist has prompted my looking with special interest for signs of John Wesley's early influence in the Capon Valley. His life (1703-1791) coincided with American colonization. The Methodist Church at Shiloh, on the Ridge east of Yellow Spring, dates back to 1800, possibly 1801.

When Bishop Lowth decided in 1780 not to ordain additional Episcopalian ministers for America, Wesley in effect usurped the power of ordination. Going further, he delegated to Methodist preachers, particularly in Virginia, the authority to ordain themselves and to administer the sacraments. In a more worldly competition, Wesley's tactics would have been counted an effective organizing maneuver.

As far as I can discover, Methodism's first standard bearer in the valley was circuit rider Francis Asbury. An Englishman, he had come to this country in 1771, when he was twenty-six years old, after being inspired at the Methodist Conference that year in Bristol by John Derby, one of Wesley's disciples, who made an impassioned plea for help in spreading Methodism to other parts of the world. Asbury responded by offering to preach to the colonies across the Atlantic. He spent the rest of his life, forty-four years, carrying the Word according to Wesley by foot and horseback to the remotest settlements and hollows from New England to the Carolinas.

A biography of Wesley, written in 1885 by Reverend B.W. Bond includes a passage about Asbury's circuit riding that offers an insight into what being a preacher on the frontier meant:

> Besides traveling and preaching, [Asbury] made it a rule to read a hundred pages daily, and to spend three hours every day in prayer. Cabins of the most miserable description were his usual homes; his daily rides were often from thirty to fifty miles over mountains and swamps, through bridgeless rivers and pathless woods, his horses weary, and he himself often cold, wet and hungry.
>
> Usually he preached at least once every week-day and thrice every Sunday. His custom was to pray with every family on whom he called in his wide wanderings. . . . For his services he received sixty-four dollars [a year] and his traveling expenses.

He rode till he could ride no longer, and then might have been seen moving about on crutches, and helped in and out of his light spring-wagon in which he continued to pursue his wanderings till he died in Baltimore in 1816. Before he died he enjoined that no life of him should be published, and to the present his injunction has been substantially observed.

This injunction was subsequently violated, to history's advantage, by the publication of *The Journals and Letters of Francis Asbury* in 1958. In an entry dated June 7, 1781, the journal reports the missionary's visit to the Capon valley: "We found some difficulty in crossing the Great Capon River. Three men very kindly carried us over in a canoe and afterward rode our horses over the stream, without fee or reward." This was probably at what is now Capon Bridge, on Asbury's way to Romney, whose inhabitants received lower marks in the missionary's chronicles. Finding them "prayerless people," he reported on June 10th: "I had about 300 people; but there were so many wicked whisky drinkers, who brought with them so much of the power of the devil, that I had little satisfaction in preaching."

By June 30th, Asbury had worked his way over the mountains to Lost River, where his complaint was equally damning but on different grounds. "The people here appear unengaged. The preaching of unconditional election, and its usual attendant Antinomianism, seems to have hardened their hearts."

Identifying antinomianism (with Noah Webster's help) as the "belief in the doctrine that faith alone, not obedience to moral law, is necessary for salvation" offers a sense of Asbury's problem. To whatever extent "whisky drinkers" had become common on the frontiers, it would have been comforting to be told on Sunday morning that Saturday night's disobedience of moral law would be absolved by faith alone. Asbury and his fellow Methodists had the organizing advantage, however, of offering salvation to all who mended their ways, in contrast to the constraints on other missionaries bound by the doctrine that immortality's prize is for only the predestined few.

Despite Asbury's efforts, the most reliable report, in a Frye family genealogy, is that "practically none of the early settlers of the Shenandoah and Capon Valley were Methodists." Inveighing against both alcohol and antinomianism may have interfered too much with local temptations and fundamentalism. Yet "at about the turn of the century," the genealogist reports, "a wave of Methodist proselytizing, replete with missionaries, camp meetings, revival services, etc. swept through the valley."

This was at the time of the historical camp meetings at Cane Ridge, Kentucky, in which Presbyterian and Methodist missionaries came together to establish a tradition of revivalist gatherings, which emphasized conversion, that swept the frontier and characterized a good deal of religious expansion in this area during the nineteenth century. A camp meeting held in 1801 or 1802 in the hollow behind the present site of the Shiloh Methodist Church went on for several months.

Less is known about the early years of the Christian Church on Timber Ridge. Its annals report that in 1811 "a minister by the name of Joseph Thomas, familiarly known as the 'White Pilgrim' came and held a meeting in a grove in a hollow just east of the present site of the church, on the Kelsoe farm. About that time a log church was erected on land donated by William Grove.

Among the early ministers who preached in the church were Isaac N. Walter, Rev. Miller, Enoch Harvey, Michael Lohr, Christy Sine, Caspar Allemong, and Simon Ward."

As part of this same religious movement, another group of area residents established the Concord Christian Church about a mile from Yellow Spring. This, too, was in a hewn-log building. The founder was "a pioneer minister by the name of Dickinson." His efforts, short-lived, are marked today by only "a few scattered graves in the old cemetery," for the Concord Christian Church joined with the Timber Ridge congregation.

This brief summary of the role religion played in unlocking the Capon valley wilderness barely suggests its impact on the region. In areas where larger settlements developed, other forces of community—town meetings, schools, business enterprises—emerged. Here there was no such commercial development and no government or education except what came with the institutions of family and church.

The missionaries' diaries bear witness to the variety of commitment the early settlers had to something higher and nobler than their own indulgence. If some paid lip service only on Sundays and chose whatever doctrines seemed convenient, many others clearly counted the Gospels' principles as imperative as the demands imposed by survival itself. Drawing their sustenance directly from the soil and their strength from faith in the Bibles they brought with them, the people who came to the valley built a legacy of equanimity and peace of mind that two centuries have left intact.

From Wilderness to Community: Homespun History

By history's common reckoning, nothing happened in Yellow Spring, West Virginia during the first half of the nineteenth century. The population doubled or tripled, but this was almost entirely by internal combustion. Few travelers and little news came in or went out. A post office was established in 1839 in the general store that Abraham Secrest added to the mill. Over the next fifteen years its revenues increased gradually to an average of about a dollar a month.

Yet history, at least as it is taught in school, is myopic. It reads and reports only headlines, leaving out the fine print about quiet developments and human happenings—raising families, enjoying health or fighting sickness, reaping bumper harvests or enduring drought-blighted fields, educating or starving children's minds—that shape ordinary individuals' lives and mold a neighborhood, which is most people's real world.

I have tried another approach to Yellow Spring history: putting together the pieces that can be found of one family's story and then tying them in with the interests and affairs they shared with their neighbors. Samuel Davis was born in 1811 on Dillon's Run, which rises on the other side of Capon Mountain, about five miles from Yellow Spring, and feeds into the river at the Bridge. Maria Swisher, eleven years younger, was the granddaughter of immigrants who settled at Intermont, near Yellow Spring, in the mid-eighteenth century. Samuel and Maria, married in 1844, lived the rest of their lives in this house where we do now. Their story is Yellow Spring's. Call it homespun history.

John R. Davis, Samuel's father, is buried in the Old Dunlap Graveyard, up on the Ridge near Lehew, beneath a brown fieldstone slab with a rough-carved inscription that can barely be made out: J.R. Davis/Died 1859/At Age 76. A broken fragment of stone beside it carries only the name Margaret.

One version of John R. Davis's lineage traces it back to a Thomas Davis who came to New Jersey from England shortly after 1700, and whose descendants included one of Hampshire County's earliest settlers, also an Elijah Davis who married Indian fighter James Caudy's daughter, and one or more certifiable Revolutionary War heroes. In this version, John's wife Margaret was born Scarff or possibly Dunlap.

The most reliable family report, however, is less dramatic. Caudy Davis put it simply: "John Davis and his wife Margaret, probably born MacMurray, came to the valley about 1805, from Scotland or England, after stopping a while in New Jersey or Pennsylvania." When I spoke to Mister Caudy later about the conflicting version, reported in a 1978 monograph by Grace Kelso Garner, he shrugged his shoulder. "I don't know," he said. "It doesn't matter." Which is right. John and Dorothy Davis Holleran confirm the simpler account in their recent and meticulously careful *Davis Genealogy*.

In any event, John and Margaret built their cabin between 1805 and 1810 along Dillon's Run. They raised three children according to family records. Samuel was the oldest; Susan, born in 1812, would live to age 105; William came along ten years later.

In 1839, Samuel left the Dillon's Run place, came over the mountain, and purchased from Joel Ellis "four hundred acres more or less" a mile below the Yellow Spring mill. This was the tract George Washington had laid out for John Lonem in 1750. The price was about $4,000, which it took Samuel a lifetime to pay off.

Maria Swisher's grandparents were John Schweitzer, who had settled in Hampshire County about 1760, and Anna Marie (Hawk) Schweitzer. Their son, John, married Elizabeth Kline, daughter of Revolutionary War Veteran Philip Klein. They had fourteen children. One of the youngest, born on April 11, 1824, was christened Mariah, but dropped her h. Her name was pronounced Mar-aye, with a trace of an r in the aye part of the name, almost but not quite "Marrar." Maria lives in local legend as a saintlike woman: relatively short and slight, attractive, always soft-spoken, usually smiling, lovely in every way.

Maria was only twenty when she and Samuel drove over to Romney on June 28, 1844 to be married. The Reverend Jacob Shump officiated at the ceremony, with James Creswell and Margaret Kline attending. They came back over the mountains to Samuel's cabin that same day or perhaps the next. Their granddaughter Lottie says that when she asked Maria once about her first reaction when she walked into her new home, Maria answered, "I remember the grandfather clock. It was directly across the room from the front door and was the first thing I saw when I came in. I thought it was the most beautiful clock in the world."

Lottie may have made this story up. It is hard to reconstruct the logistics of a grandfather clock making its way to the Capon Valley before 1844. Other fragments of family memory suggest that the fifty-year-old cabin Samuel brought Maria to was plain and simply furnished. The front door, then on the mountain side of the cabin, opened into a room dominated by a large stone fireplace on the wall to the right. An enclosed staircase just to the left of the door divided this part of the first floor from Samuel and Maria's bedroom. The upstairs was partitioned into four small rooms.

The living that went on in the cabin was plain. New members were added to the Davis cast at what must have sometimes seemed monotonous year-and-a-half to two-year intervals. Everybody beyond the age of five spent six full days a week, but never on Sunday, at hard labor. Education was in a century-long recess. There were two little worlds here, one male, one female; not entirely separate, clearly not equal.

There was special exultation in the Davis cabin at the appearance of first son John William on May 5, 1845 and appropriate if more casual applause for Mary Catherine on September 11, 1846. George Franklin (March 11, 1848) would become Tom and Caudy Davis's father. In twenty-three years, Maria produced the cut-rate dozen, of whom eight grew to maturity. Necessity led Samuel to add two rooms to the back of the house.

The record of Samuel's capacity for hard work is clear. In addition to farming his fifty or sixty acres of tillable fields and pasture, he carried on a tanning operation set up below the spring north of the cabin, and built and operated a leatherworking shop, which was just across the lane from the house. Yet he had a hard time making ends meet, and had to sell off several pieces of his land.

Caudy Davis once summarized his grandfather's life. "He worked awfully hard, but he was always poor. So was everybody else. There just wasn't ever any money in this part of the valley."

Granddaughter Lottie, who died in 1986 at age 101, recalled Maria (in whose home Lottie did her growing up, most of it after Samuel's death in 1888) as an extraordinary woman. "She was the hardest working person any of us ever knew, but she never seemed to mind. Every floor in the house got scrubbed with sand two or three times a year, and the curtains never got dirty. She was the reason everybody went to church every Sunday. And she gave her children all the education they ever got. It took with the girls but not with the boys. She didn't say an unkind word in her life."

The reference to education stands out in Lottie's silhouette of her grandmother. The single most telling factor in the story of Yellow Spring, 1800-1860, is that during this period most valley children learned less about reading, writing, and arithmetic than their ancestors had brought with them when they had settled here a hundred years earlier.

Attributing this lapse of learning to something in

Appalachian genes would be wrong. Virginia's tide-water aristocrats had decided to do virtually nothing for boys and girls whose parents couldn't afford private education. In 1857, the Commonwealth had less than a fifth as many children in public school as did smaller Massachusetts and New Hampshire, a tenth the number in even less populated Illinois. This policy of deliberate educational starvation was particularly directed at the mountain areas west of the Blue Ridge. The western settlers, who had followed routes from Europe different from those that had brought immigrants to Richmond, were looked down on. The mountaineers were also too poor to pay state taxes. Although Romney, the Hampshire county seat, became a remarkable center of locally supported educational and literary activity, this was a notable exception. Historians H. Maxwell and H.L. Swisher report in their 1895 *History of Hampshire* that in the rest of the entire county in 1860 there were "no more than eight or ten small, crude and poorly finished public school buildings."

A one-room school was built and maintained for a time in the 1820s near Hooks Mill, just below Yellow Spring, with the redoubtable George Nicholas Spaid, Hessian emeritus, serving as a teacher. Some winter classes were also held for a few months in the school-rooms that had been included in Shiloh Methodist Church and at the Lutheran Church. Sandy Grove School, near Concord, and Lafayette School, two or three miles below the Yellow Spring mill, functioned sporadically.

Itinerant teachers occasionally came to live for a few months during the winter with one family or another, trading their meager knowledge of the three Rs for room and board and a few dollars collected in the neigh-

borhood. But this was off any usual route even for rov-
ing pedagogues, and what few dollars got together had
to go for too many other things. Yellow Spring didn't
really start school until it was a hundred years old.

When I asked Caudy Davis what effect this educational starvation had, he shook his head slowly, an-
swering then with an earthy and apt metaphor. "It was
like not putting manure or lime on your land. The crops
came up but they were stunted. It was a terrible thing."

I asked if there was any reading in Samuel and
Maria's home. "A little," Mister Caudy answered. "Not
much."

"Were there newspapers or magazines?"

"No, probably not. There weren't many published
then, and they cost money."

The Hampshire and Hardy Intelligencer had been
established in Romney in 1830 by William Harper.
Changing its name to the *South Branch Intelligencer,*
by 1850 the weekly built up its readership in the two
counties to about a thousand, probably none of them
in remote Yellow Spring.

"How about books?"

Mister Caudy thought a moment. "Not many. There
was a bookshelf with ten or fifteen books on it. The
Bible, of course. I don't remember the others. The almanac hung by a little loop of string at the end of the
shelf."

Looking through the mid-nineteenth-century volumes on the bookshelf beside my desk, gleanings from
box-and-contents purchases at local estate sales, permits guessing at what kinds of books Samuel and
Maria's little library included. Most of them probably
related to religion.

They might have had a copy of *Line Upon Line, or*

a Second Series of the Earliest Religious Instruction the Infant Mind is Capable of Receiving. My copy, lacking a publication date but obviously old, is inscribed "Hebron Sabbath School." The copy I have of *The Christian's Manual, A Treatise on Christian Perfection; with Direction for Obtaining the State* (1853) belonged to William I. Frye, of Wardensville. Valentine Secrest's and Samuel Brill's names are inside the cover of S. S. Schmucker's 1856 volume, *American Lutheranism Vindicated; or Examination of the Lutheran Symbols, on Certain Disputed Topics: Including a Reply to the Plea of Rev. W.J. Mann.* A good many of these religious publications—for example *The True Boy: Obstacles Well Met, and Ultimate Triumph* (1857, anonymous), and *Religion and Eternal Life or Irreligion and Perpetual Ruin* (1834), by J.C. Pike—were published by the American Tract Society.

There would have been a hymnal among the Davises' few volumes, for no box of old books ever shows up at an estate auction without a collection of church songs. I have Samuel Frye's worn copy of *A Collection of Hymns for the Use of the Methodist Episcopal Church, Principally from the Collection of the Rev. John Wesley,* published in 1821. The earliest publications included only the hymns' words, without music, permitting the printing of as many as eight hundred hymns in what were sometimes very small volumes, two inches wide, three inches high, and an inch-and-a-half thick. Although one little book identifies this as an economy measure, there was also a time when singing in church was considered sacrilegious.

Mister Caudy remembered that his grandparents had an almanac on their bookshelf. Probably J. Gruber's

Hagerstown Town and Country Almanack, first published in 1797, it was unquestionably the second-most-relied-upon volume, after the Bible, up and down the valley. Although potatoes were always put in on Good Friday, rain or shine, all other agricultural operations from planting to harvest were carried out "according to the signs" as they were set out on a 365-day-to-day basis in the almanac.

I had assumed that planting by the signs depended on a combination of knowledge and instinct handed down from generation to generation. Not at all. Mr. Gruber provides instant and easy access to the occult. Using the 1851 *Hagerstown Almanack* here on my desk, its corners worn more from previous thumbing than from time, I can decide readily—as of Friday evening, April 18 of that year—whether to plant the garden the next day. By no means, for Saturday the 19th is listed on the almanac calendar as under the sign of Sagittarius, "a Fiery, Masculine sign . . . not a favorable time to plant or transplant." But Sunday, the 20th and Monday, the 21st will fall under Capricorn, "a Moist Movable sign that will produce a rapid growth of pulp, stalks or roots." Consulting Gruber's "Conjecture of the Weather for each Day," I find that Sunday will be clear, Monday "changeable," with a likelihood of rain on the next three days. Respecting the Sabbath, seeking Capricorn's blessing, and wanting to get my seed in before the rain, I go for Monday.

Lumber was sawed according to Mr. Gruber's specifications. It was well known that cutting it under a threatening juxtaposition of constellations greatly increased the risks of warpage.

All mysticism? I was surer of this before Charley Alger, who helped us do some things when we moved here in 1968, including putting in a well, checked me out as a certifiable dowser. Telling Jane one morning where he had located the underground water source, he showed me how to hold the dowser's forked willow stick and put me to covering the broad area between the back of the house and the mountain. After several minutes of totally skeptical meandering, I suddenly felt the stick pull down so sharply that it hurt my wrists. Looking over at them, I saw Charley doubled up laughing and Jane in shock. I was at the precise spot he had told her about. As for planting by the signs, our extraordinarily well-informed friend Mary Massey, who has green thumbs on both hands, wouldn't think of planting a seed—or the corkscrew willow she put in beside the stile leading to our pond—without consulting the almanac.

By fortuitous circumstance, Samuel Davis—in whose home there were no newspapers or magazines and only "ten or fifteen books"—turned out to be himself a contributor to Yellow Spring's literature and a chronicler of its history. He kept, and his grandson Caudy preserved, a day-to-day ledger of his leather-working business, starting in 1839. Later, serving as local constable for five years during the 1850s, he again kept meticulous records. Both the cobbler's ledger and the constable's logbook are here on my desk.

At first glance, the items in the ledger seem sterile—customers' names, services rendered, prices charged. Yet a surprising number of these names from a hundred and fifty years ago are still familiar in the valley: Anderson, Brill, Casper, Dunlap, Frye, Hiett, Himelwright, Kline, LaFollette, Lupton, Orndorff, Peacemaker, Pennington, Rudolph, Slonaker, Spaid,

Switzer. Yellow Spring roots reach deep. And reading between the lines, after unscrambling the spelling (Samuel Davis would have agreed with his president, Andrew Jackson, that "anybody who can't spell a word at least two ways isn't worth a damn"), reveals quite a bit about mid-eighteenth century Yellow Spring ways of doing business and living.

This more careful reading also suggests why the cobbler never had much money. Each customer is identified as "Dr"—for Debtor; most business was done on credit, with settlement to be made at harvest time. Payments were frequently in produce. Receipts totaled between a third and a half of the charges listed, probably depending on how well the weather served the crops.

Samuel's first customer, in May of 1839, was Lemuel Pugh, whom the cobbler charged "12½ cents to patching on boots" and thirty-three cents for "half-soling one pare shoes." Lemuel, like everybody else in the valley, was long on lineage but short on cash. A descendant of the Pughs who had done business along the Great Cacapehon with surveyor Washington in April 1750, Lemuel didn't get around to his 45½ cent bill until 1841.

Cobbler Davis did business with twelve customers his first year, over two-thirds of it with the Carter and Lee families. Of the $161.43 he put on the books, he had collected about forty-five dollars by the end of December. Some more dribbled in during the following year, mostly in produce.

The shoemaker developed several sidelines, perhaps partly because he had to liquidate the payments he received in barter, possibly as a reflection of the variety of his talents. The January 4, 1840 listing of a transaction with "Mongumory Ellison" includes, along with several cobblery items ("To mending one pare of shoes—18¢" and "To one pare of shoes—$2.00"), three others: "To half pound of tobacco—16¢; To 26 lbs. of flower—91¢; To half gallon of whisky—25¢."

Customer S. Beckwith's 1840 account included the purchase of three bushels of oats at fifteen cents a bushel, "3 Dozen of fish—27½ cents," and an item "To brandy 12½ cents" that reveals nothing about quantity, quality, or source. David Brooks paid fifty cents a bushel for corn in 1843. In 1844, customers William McKay and John Frank worked off part of their bills at thirty-three cents or fifty cents a day, depending on the kind of work they did in the shoemaker's fields.

Over the next decade, the charge for Davis footwear remained about the same but other prices, especially for grain, moved up. In 1856, customer George W. Blake bought, in addition to shoes, two-and-a-half bushels of wheat for $3.25, bacon at ten cents a pound, potatoes at fifty cents a bushel, coffee at fourteen cents a pound, and a gallon of whiskey for 72½ cents. He took care of part of his bill by "thrashing wry $1.00," sawing a tree for fifty cents, "plowing, 87¢," and working one day "self and boy 75¢."

An ordinary entry in the cobbler's daybook—"April 20, 1841. Westfall Fry. 2 Bushels of Corn $1.87"—becomes one line in a story that can be traced back over two-and-a-half centuries. Henry Westfall Frye was a grandson of the Henry Frye who had come to the valley in the 1750s. Jane and I spent a delightful afternoon in 1984 visiting, along with our close friends Ben and Elizabeth Frye, the still-pert-and-vivacious-at-ninety Pauline Warden (Polly) Wertz who lived until her death the next year on what was originally

Henry Frye's, and then customer Westfall's, property. Polly's family lines included both the Fryes and the Wardens of Wardensville. As she showed us the handsome walnut corner cupboard that was once patriarch Henry's and probably Westfall's, the centuries seemed only minutes.

The cobbler's moonlighting as constable, from 1853 to 1858, put Samuel Davis in the service of three justices of the peace, George Spaid, Samuel Milslagle, and one of the Nixons from Capon Bridge. The constable and justice of the peace titles suggest a considerable exposure to the seamy side of local law and order. The list of fees provided by the law of the times for a constable's services included "for putting a condemned man in the stocks, twenty-one cents; for shipping a slave, to be paid by the master, twenty-one cents; for removing a person likely to become a charge on the county per mile, four cents."

Yet only a handful of the several hundred items in Constable Davis's record involved miscreants brought to justice for untoward or felonious deeds. The justices' and constables' principal function was to enforce the local credit system. Money was seasonal in the valley, coming in only at harvest time. Since most transactions during the year were covered by IOUs, disagreements often developed about the terms of the debt; or if the harvest was disappointing, arrangements had to be made to extend the period for repayment. Differences that couldn't be settled were taken to a justice of the peace.

Although the amounts of money involved were usually small, frequently as little as $1.50 or $2.00, the proceedings were conducted with a formality that was

critical to their effectiveness. Bringing a claim before
the J.P. resulted, when the facts were established, in
the issuance of a solemn document of "execution."

> Hampshire County, to wit: To Samuel Davis, Constable
> of the said county:
> I command you, in the name of the Commonwealth of
> Virginia, that of the goods and chattels of John Pea-
> cemaker in your district, you cause to be made the sum
> of four Dollars and 57½ Cents, with interest thereon
> from the 15th day of October 1856, till paid, which Ellis
> Lupton has recovered before me, in a warrant in debt,
> and also the sum of no dollars and 30 Cents, which was
> adjudged to the said E. Lupton for prosecuting his said
> Warrant.
> Given under my hand this 16th day of June 1857
> George Spaid, J.P.

The constable took it from there. Peacemaker, like
most debtors, paid up. At this point, the constable received his commission of thirty cents.

If the execution didn't bring satisfaction, the creditor
would come before the J.P. again, and unless sufficient
assurance was provided, a more formidable "judgment"
would issue. Justice of the Peace Samuel Milslagle's
decree in the 1856 matter of a debt by Peter Farmer
and John W. Eaton in the amount of twenty-seven dollars to one James Mullikan provided that "one horse,
the property of the above bound Peter Farmer, is now
in the custody of Samuel Davis . . . to be held by him
until payment of the debt plus 6 per cent interest per
annum and costs for the Constable of Thirty Cents."

Although defendant Farmer tried to cover his obli-
gations, making a payment of $2.50 on August 4, 1856,
his efforts proved futile. A slip of paper in the account
book records the constable's additional receipt from

Farmer on April 17, 1858 "as security" of "One Safe, $7.00; One Beauro $7.00; One Bed and Beading $8.00; Four head of hogs $6.00."

While Constable Davis's records don't make clear what eventually happened to Farmer's chattels, another entry records a "sail of property" conducted by the constable to satisfy Isaac Brill's claim against M. Capper; a bridle brought $2.15, a bay mare and saddle $12.50, "I Waggon" $11.00, and the family cooking stove $20.50. Although this was more a matter of enforcing a system of credit than of keeping the peace, justice had sharp teeth.

The results were happier in the case of a May 1858 indebtedness of $21.75 running from James Slonaker and Jacob Swisher to B. F. Frye. After putting up as security "one black cow and one cooking stove," Slonaker and Swisher paid off their debt, plus 6 percent interest, the following August. The indicated waiver of any constabulary commission on this transaction may reflect the kinship between debtor Swisher and the constable's wife.

The justices of the peace were also the local probate officers, settling estates. Constable Davis reported "an execution Agst George Carlyle in favour of John Kline" covering an indebtedness of twenty dollars. The settlement was acknowledged by "David Pugh, Adm of John Kline, Dec'd." Justice moved slowly even in those days: Administrator Pugh's claim was dated October of 1846, the settlement January 18, 1855.

Wondering about the reason for a sharp fall off in cobbler Davis's business in 1849 and 1850, I think I know the answer. That was the period when two major construction projects were underway in the valley.

One was the building of the new Lutheran Church at Intermont. All of the work was done by members of the parish. Samuel and Maria were active communicants, and Samuel undoubtedly spent a good many hours helping build the church.

Early in the century, the original hewn-log structure at Intermont had been moved across the road to pemit laying out a cemetery in the sandy loam just above the river; this made for easier burials during the winter months when the soil was frozen. The new brick church was built beside the cemetery.

The moving spirits throughout the construction were pastors X.J. Richardson and Peter Miller. Their annual salaries of $400 were paid partially in wheat, corn, pork, beef, chickens, and potatoes; partly from the proceeds of church suppers that are still among the area's popular attractions; and partly, the church's annual records reveal, not at all.

The work on the new building went on for seven or eight years. Clay for the bricks was dug from a bed just south of the building and fired in a kiln set up beside the cemetery. Ben Anderson did the interior woodwork. But some money was required and there was very little available. Work went ahead until the funds were exhausted and then stopped for a period of months. Wilbur Brill reports his Aunt Bessie's passing on the account of Pastor Richardson's continued exhortation. "He said 'we have got to build the church' and they said 'we can't possibly do it.' And he just pushed them right into it and they got agoing doing it." (Today Kathleen Good keeps up the tradition of planting an extra piece of garden each year to produce vegetables for the Saturday night public dinners, the same church suppers that once provided part of the money for paying the pastor and building the church.)

Samuel almost certainly put in a lot of time, too, on the construction of the huge new hotel that was being built at Watson Town, up Capon Spring Hollow, three miles through the woods from the Yellow Spring mill. The pay there was fifty cents a day. In cash. Samuel couldn't afford to pass it up.

The hotel story goes back, by familiar account, to Henry Frye's discovering an artesian spring when he killed a bear one day in the mid-1760s. Impressed with the pure taste and pleasant coolness (sixty-four degrees) and flow (6,000 gallons an hour) of the spring, Henry reportedly brought his wife Fanny, who suffered from swollen joints, back with him to test the Indian legend that the water cured "the rheumatiz." Delighted with the results, they built their cabin close by.

When word of these natural wonders got around, nine local men joined Henry Frye in getting authority from the state legislature at Richmond to lay out and sell lots in the twenty-acre area around the spring "from whence the water issues, supposed efficacious in certain disorders." As a condition of taking title to a lot under the 1787 statute granted to Frye, a purchaser had to build a dwelling house at least sixteen feet square with a brick or stone chimney.

The business venture proved less efficacious than the water. A new set of trustees was appointed by the legislature in 1800, to be succeeded by still another in 1816. A fourth enactment, in 1830, reflected continuing difficulty. Historian Kercheval's 1833 report was that "there are seventeen or eighteen houses erected without much regard to regularity, and a boarding establishment, capable of accommodating fifty or sixty visitors, which is kept in excellent style." The settlement, known first as Watson Town, was later renamed Capon Springs.

Then, in 1849, the Baltimore firm of Buck, Blake-
more, and Ricord built The Mountain House. Described
as the largest and most impressive watering place in
the country, its dining hall seated 600 people. The Virginia legislature appropriated $20,000 to establish the
baths, repayment to be made by the proprietors out of
the revenues.

The valley's second most historied moment, a hundred
years after the Washington surveys, came in June of
1851 when Daniel Webster, then Secretary of State in
President Millard Fillmore's cabinet, came out to speak
at the new hotel, bringing with him the British Am-
bassador Sir Henry Bulwer. Webster used the occasion
to give the kickoff speech in his campaign for the 1852
Democratic nomination for the presidency. He had gotten in trouble with the antislavery Northerners by col-
laborating with Henry Clay, "the great compromiser,"
in the 1850 enactment of the fugitive slave law. Winchester's leading Democrat, William L. Clarke, felt
that this borderline area between North and South
would be a good place for the candidate to mend fences.

Webster spent two-and-a-half hours at it, standing
on one of the dining-room tables and holding his au-
dience spellbound. He summarized his remarks in an
August 1, 1851 letter to a North Carolina correspond-
ent: "What I said at Capon Springs was an argument
addressed to the North, and intended to convince the
North that if, by its superiority in numbers, it shall
defeat the operation of a plain, undoubted, and unde-
niable injunction of the Constitution, intended for the
especial protection of the South, such a proceeding
must necessarily end in the breaking up of the Government, that is to say, in a revolution." He would be
proved tragically right.

Part of Capon Springs lore, consistent with Webster's reputed acquaintance with strong spirits, involves another speech he made the following day, dedicating the new hotel swimming pool. Gesturing toward the small body of water beside which the assemblage had gathered, the slightly hung-over orator opened his remarks: "As we stand here on the banks of the beautiful Severn. . . ."

On leaving the hotel, the Secretary of State wrote a letter of thanks, addressed to "H.M. Brent, Esq., President of the Board of Trustees of Watson Town":

> My Dear Sir: I cannot leave these Springs without communicating, through you, to the Trustees of Watson Town, my cordial thanks for their unanimous resolution, so respectful to myself, presented to me on my arrival. Personally unknown to the gentlemen who compose your Board, I yet do not feel myself to be an alien or a stranger among them, or among any others of my fellow citizens who, like them, manifest a strong attachment to the Union of the States.

Webster went on to salute the hotel as "second to none within my knowledge for the purposes designed for it . . . and surrounded by beautiful scenery."

Despite the good sense of Webster's remarks in his formal speech, both his candidacy and the hotel proprietors' new venture faced uncertain and eventually frustrated futures. The Democratic nomination went to Franklin Pierce, "a Northern man with Southern principles." As it turned out, Daniel Webster died two weeks before the 1852 election. The hotel did well at first. Rates were an attractive forty dollars a month for room and meals, "children under ten and colored servants half price." But by the end of the decade, the trustees found themselves $8,000 in debt, and as war clouds gathered, the hotel closed.

The hotel reopened in the late 1860s under the proprietorship of Messrs. Frazier and Sale and prospered sufficiently that an annex was added to the Mountain House in 1887. By the turn of the century, however, the geographical remoteness which has always been one of the area's shaping forces closed in on the enterprise. Guests had to take the Valley Branch of the Baltimore & Ohio from Harpers Ferry to Strasburg and then travel fifteen miles by wagon coach over North Mountain. What had been tolerable inconvenience before began to seem disproportionate; the automobile and decent roads came about ten years too late. The hotel's mounting troubles culminated in an insurance fire in 1912 that destroyed the original building, but left the 1887 annex and the baths and some of the outside guest quarters standing.

Twenty years later, in the mid-1930s, two extraordinary people, Lou and Virginia Austin, bought the property at a tax sale and began reconstructing an inn of uniquely informal and friendly character, which prospers today under their grandchildren's operation. Whatever Capon Springs water did for Fanny Frye's rheumatism two centuries ago, the spring and its stewards provide tranquillity and peace of mind today for thousands of families.

Even the social historians, looking behind headline events, would find hardly a flutter on their registers of Yellow Spring development during the eighty years between the wars, Revolutionary and Civil. If the infant mortality rate in the valley dropped a little, and people's average longevity increased by a few months, the differences were slight. It was a no-growth period as far as education was concerned. The ratio between back-bending labor and the luxury of leisure stayed about the same. The readings on the "per capita income" and "family savings" barometers didn't vary, remaining at or slightly below zero.

It is true and important that where there had been a wilderness at the beginning of this period, a few families living in virtual isolation, a community had developed. The three churches contributed substantially to this. People were doing together a good many things they had previously done alone. Yet with virtually no lines of communication or transportation having developed, and with education remaining dormant, Yellow Spring 1860 was not very different from what it had been when Samuel Davis and Maria Swisher first knew it.

That everything had remained so much the same in the valley, so quiet for so long, made it impossible to accept the portents of change and total disruption that started shaping up after mid-century. Standing beside the Yellow Spring mill and looking toward North Mountain, just four miles to the east, it was inconceivable that this ridge would be part of the boundary line between two halves of a country at war with itself, and that the Capon Valley would be a tormented no-man's-land in a fratricidal conflict.

Rebellion Against Rebellion
Against Rebellion

An amateur historian from north of the Mason-Dixon line runs into trouble trying to unravel the most critical piece of Capon Valley history. I remembered from American History I in high school that West Virginia was carved out of the Old Dominion at the start of the Civil War because the higher-principled mountaineers refused to go along with Virginia's slaveholding tidewater secessionists. But, sixty years later, I was in a West Virginia community whose strongest traditions trace back to its having fought for the Confederacy. It was confusing.

Part of the problem was my unthinking assumption that all settlers came to the valley of their own free will and from north of the Equator. Mountaineering and slaveholding seemed inherently incongruous.

I was wrong. Virginia's first census, the 1782 State Enumeration, reported 454 slaves in Hampshire County, one for every fifteen whites. The black population increased to 1,443 by 1850. In his 1794 will, Jonathan Pugh, Capon Valley pioneer, bequeathed "to my loving wife Margaret . . . two negroes Dick and Trusty for her life." After Benjamin Frye's death in 1840, the appraisers of his estate—including Abraham Secrest, owner of the mill and Yellow Spring's recently appointed postmaster—listed seven slaves; their value ranged from "$1 (negro woman named Leah 65 or 70 years of age)" to "$400 (negro girl named Rachel 10 years old)." When the Lutherans built their new church at Intermont in the late 1840s, they included a small balcony at the back to permit the equal but separate devotions of the communicants' slaves.

It isn't clear whether Samuel and Maria Davis were slaveholders. Their grandson Caudy remembered hearing that they were, and that the jumbled fieldstones lying fifty feet north of our house around a slightly warm spring were part of the foundation for a shanty Samuel built for a slave couple, putting it over the spring to keep the occupants a little warmer in the winter. Caudy's nephew Forrest questions the report. His logic (that no Davis ever had enough money to buy a slave) and alternative explanation for the fieldstones (that they were there to keep the cattle from falling into the spring) are bolstered by the 1850 Census Report in the National Archives. It lists Samuel Davis (farmer; age 38; property value $2,500), Maria, their first four children, and a "Charles W. Frank, laborer" as members of the household; but no slaves are included. It was the census takers' usual practice to include slaves if any lived on the premises.

There is no question, though, about the Davis view on secession. When Samuel and Maria's tenth child was born, on January 29, 1861, he was named Jefferson. A week earlier, the Virginia legislature had passed the key secession resolution and another Jefferson Davis was emerging as titular head of the Confederacy.

If this was slaveholding and secession-minded territory, how did it happen that it became part of the new state—first called Kanawha (for the territory's principal river) and then officially West Virginia—established in protest against Virginia's insistence on adhering to the Constitutional decree that some people are born only three-fifths equal? Nobody here seemed to know. So I picked up another puzzle.

I expected to find the explanation in historians Hu Maxwell and H.L. Swisher's 1897 *History of Hampshire County*. But they include only a single cryptic paragraph.

> When the [new West Virginia] constitution was framed, it did not regard Hampshire, Hardy, Pendleton, and Morgan [counties] as part of the state, but provided that they might become parts of West Virginia if they voted in favor of adopting the constitution. They so voted, and thus came into the state.

But why did people here vote one way when they were about to march off, as they did a few weeks later, in another?

The story is told, as far as I can discover, only in two little-known and out-of-print volumes: the Festus P. Summers 1939 account of *The Baltimore and Ohio in the Civil War*, and Alvin Edward Moore's *History of Hardy County, of the Borderland,* published in 1963. The clue to it all is in the title of the Summers book. The critical fact behind that vote that made Hampshire

County part of West Virginia was that seventy-five miles of the mainline of the Baltimore and Ohio Railroad ran along the county's northern boundary, on the south side of the Potomac.

Bruce Caton provides the basis for understanding what happened in his classic 1961 *The Coming Fury*. "To go west from Washington it was necessary to use the Baltimore and Ohio Railroad and this road lay almost completely at Virginia's mercy. . . . To the people of Ohio this was a matter of great importance. They not only wanted direct communication with the national capital; even more they wanted to be able to send their produce to the Western market at Baltimore. Since Ohio was the most populous state in the West, and had furnished most of McClellan's troops, Ohio could make its wishes felt." Which it did, bringing the Hampshire County section of the B&O into the Union by a procedure that would embarrass all but the most cynical practitioner of politic's darker arts.

The fuller record confirms that the architects of the new state, meeting in Wheeling at various times during 1861, came to the democratic conclusion that the drawing of West Virginia's boundaries should be left up to a series of county-by-county referendums. Yet they knew that the residents of Hampshire would vote overwhelmingly to stay with Virginia, which would mean that a critical stretch of the B&O mainline would be outside Union control. The representatives of the military industrial complex sitting in Wheeling stayed with the referendum principle. But some funny things happened to democracy on the way to the polls in Hampshire County.

The crucial vote came at the county elections for the delegates to the convention in Wheeling that was to adopt the boundary selection procedures. Historian Moore describes the peculiar credentials of the two delegates from Confederate-minded Hampshire County. George Washington Sheets, twenty-seven years old and a former employee of the B&O, had been comissioned by Francis H. Pierpont, principal organizer of the movement to establish a new state, "to recruit militia for the defense of the railroad." The other Hampshire delegate, T. R. Carskadon, "was an idealist and reformer . . . He had advocated the abolition of slavery to the point of having to flee from Virginia for his life."

At the December 13, 1861 session of the convention, idealist Carskadon felt compelled at one point to explain how he and Sheets had become delegates. "We have about 14 precincts in our county. We opened the polls at two precincts . . . I was at New Creek [one of the two] during the whole two days election . . . There was not over 39 votes cast of citizens of that vicinity who had a right to vote for delegates for the convention."

It turns out that former B&O employee George Washington Sheets had done his job thoroughly. The Hampshire County "election" had been restricted to the precincts at Piedmont, on the mainline of the railroad in the county's northwest corner, and at New Creek, four miles from Piedmont. Bringing in Union soldiers to do the voting, it came out 179 in favor and 16 against the two delegates supporting the new state. Historian Summers reports that similar procedures in neighboring Hardy County produced a vote of 150 to 0, and that no elections at all were held in the three other counties—Morgan, Berkeley, and Jefferson—which were eventually included in the new state despite their residents' predominant pro-Confederacy sentiment.

The First General Assembly, held at Wheeling in July, recognized abolitionist Carskadon as the senator from Hampshire, Hardy, and Morgan counties. The charade continued with an election on May 22, 1862 at which Pierpont was selected as governor of the new state; no votes were recorded from Hampshire or Hardy in this mandate.

When the Constitutional Convention voted the new state's boundaries and certified its action to the national Congress in Washington, Hampshire and the other four counties were included. Congress voted to admit the new state. Advised by three of his cabinet members that the whole procedure was unconstitutional and improper, President Lincoln hesitated but finally signed the bill on December 31, 1862. He observed in his accompanying message that "there is difference enough between secession against the Constitution and secession in favor of the Constitution. I believe the admission of West Virginia to the Union is expedient."

Although the admission statute required still another county-by-county vote approving the new state constitution, Sheets and Carskadon again proved equal to the demand. The referendum was held in Hampshire on March 26, 1863. The number of eligible voters in the county was in the thousands. There is no record of how the election was conducted or any other detail except the officially reported results: seventy-five votes for inclusion in the new state, nine against.

Similar shenanigans practiced in four other border counties—Berkeley, Hardy, Jefferson, and Morgan—were subsequently brought before the Supreme Court of the United States in an 1870 case entitled *Virginia v. West Virginia.* After setting out the facts in only partial but incriminating detail, Mr. Justice Samuel F. Miller concluded for a bare majority of the Court:

> Are we to go behind all this and inquire as to what took place at the voting? To inquire how many votes were actually cast? . . . All of these and many more embarrassing questions must arise if the Court is to go into the allegations.

So the Court didn't. The dead and defeated past was left to bury its political refuse.

An embittered Confederate, T.S. Wade, chaplain of the Nineteenth Volunteer Virginia Cavalry, was less restrained than Justice Miller: "They call the new state 'The Child of the Storm.' It is a war baby all right—the bastard offspring of a political rape." Genealogist Bess Lorentz Wade, reporting the chaplain's pungent remark in her 1968 family chronicle *Lest We Forget*, also comments on the fact that the original West Virginia constitution was unique in leaving out the name of God. "One cannot but wonder," Ms. Wade goes on, "if the omission was not caused for the reason that the Deity was not consulted on that occasion." (The flaw was cured by constitutional amendment in 1960.)

In retrospect it is hard to see what was gained by the ballot box frauds. No allegiances were changed; when West Virginia seceded from Virginia because Virginia seceded from the Union, the five counties seceded in effect from West Virginia. Historian Maxwell names several hundred men from Hampshire County who enlisted in thirteen Confederate companies. Only a handful put on blue uniforms. The fighting throughout the war at Harpers Ferry and all along the B&O mainline and spurs wasn't materially affected by the technicality that they ran through nominally Union territory.

I don't understand, either, why sentiment and conviction in Hampshire and the other four border counties was so strong in support of secession and the Confederacy. Along with residents of the other mountain counties farther west, people here resented the Virginia legislature's crippling discrimination that denied them public funds for roads and schools. It is hard to imagine any intense feeling in the Capon Valley about states rights as a philosophical issue. What brief historical commentary I have found suggests that it did come down to a proslavery position. The 1860 census report shows that 8½ percent of the population in the five counties was "negro". Ownership has always meant a great deal here, partly because not many people have ever owned very much. So perhaps the economics of taking people's slaves away from them was clearer than the moral issue; it made equal rights wrong. I just don't know.

In any event, loyalties in the valley were undivided. Yellow Spring accounts of the war include nothing of brothers fighting brothers. The names on the "Annual Consolidated Return of the Strength of the Eleventh Regiment of the Virginia Militia"—Jacob Baker, Morgan Brill, George Frye, John Himelright, Robert Hook, Jonathan Lupton, Robert Oats, Joseph Perrell, Solomon Rosbrough, William Slonaker, Francis Spaid—suggest that it was recruited along the Capon. Jacob Warden and Joseph Godlove were officers in Company I of the Eighteenth Virginia Cavalry, and its roster included John Kline, Tilbury and Jacob and

John Orndorff, Jacob Rudolph, Anthony Reed, Benjamin McKeever, Jason Frye, John and Nicholas Heishman, Benjamin and Simon Swisher. Others from along the river (including John W. Davis) were with the Frontier Riflemen in the Thirteenth Virginia Infantry. But any such listing is unfair to those it leaves out. Virtually every able-bodied male in the valley between the ages of sixteen and fifty marched or rode to the Stars and Bars.

Trying to bring into focus what the war was like in the Yellow Spring area, more generally in Hampshire County, produces a picture that seems mockingly unreal. Both Romney, twenty-five miles west, and Winchester, equally close to the east, were centers of the conflict. Romney changed hands between Confederate and Union troops fifty-six times, Winchester seventy-eight. Stonewall Jackson's 1862 resignation, later withdrawn, was caused by his disgust when the Confederate Secretary of War ordered him to have General Loring evacuate Romney; and on the Union side, it was at Romney that Captain Martin (Lew) Wallace distinguished himself long before he wrote *Ben Hur*. Three major battles were fought in and around Winchester, in May of 1862, June of 1863, and September of 1864.

The natural inference from this is that the nearby Capon Valley was constantly afire throughout the war, a no-man's-land defying normal activity. Yet the only report by historians Maxwell and Swisher of even a skirmish in the Yellow Spring area is a brief reference to "an engagement at Timber Ridge, August 1, 1863." They also tell of a notorious "organized band of thieves and robbers with headquarters on Timber Ridge, who did not belong to either army, and were outlawed by both . . . despised by the soldiers and dreaded by the citizens." These were probably the "bush-whackers" who stopped Abraham Frye on December 8, 1864 as he was driving a wagon loaded with farm products from Yellow Spring to Winchester, demanded that he turn the produce over to them, and then killed him when he resisted.

Most of the fighting that took place in Hampshire County was a strange kind of dueling with deadly weapons, resulting occasionally in a fatality but essentially a macabre side show. Most of those changes of control at Romney were matters of a few blue-uniformed cavalry riding into town, occupying the county building (burning it once), and then withdrawing when word came that a slightly larger number of "Rebs" were moving in. Two of the changes occurred the same day, without a shot being fired.

The weird character that war took on is reflected in the story, which appears in too many reports to permit its being dismissed as anecdotage, of the Hampshire County official records. It was natural enough that the deed books and those containing the records of wills and the settlement of estates were moved out of the Romney courthouse by County Clerk White and his son, who was a Confederate captain, and taken to Winchester for safer keeping; and that they had to be moved again, when Winchester was threatened, to a cave near Luray. But it is hard to understand the decision of some Union soldiery to go after them there, or to explain the skirmish in which the blue uniformed defenders of national integrity were caught by Captain White and his men in the act of defacing the Hampshire records by resort to defecatious maneuvers not recognized in the Articles of War. Having suffered only minor damage, the documents were gotten off to North Carolina, to be returned to Romney after Appomattox.

The worst blight of the war on the valley itself was the ravaging of barns and kitchens and food cellars by Union troops moving through in seeming aimlessness. Caudy Davis remembered the stories of what happened when word came that the Feds were approaching. "The shoes and boots in the shop were hidden in a secret hole down under one of the walls. The good saddles were stashed away in barrels and covered with trash. The horses were driven up onto the mountain. The Feds knew about the horses, but they also knew that two or three of the boys were up there, waiting with rifles for anybody who tried to climb the path or scramble up the rocks."

The imbalance between fighting and foraging is described vividly, from a Union perspective, in a diary kept by Gordon R. Powell, with the Eighty-Seventh Pennsylvania Regiment, on an expedition between Petersburg and Capon Springs in December of 1862.

> Petersburg was the most forlorn looking town the boys had yet seen in West Virginia. Everything was in a dilapidated condition. All ablebodied men were in the Confederate Army. The women, boys and old men gazed reproachfully at the 'Yanks' as [we] marched through the town . . .
>
> Scouting parties were sent out in search of the enemy. Foraging was supposed to be prohibited, but the officers did not prevent it. A captain saw one of his men come into camp with a ham on his back and one under his arm . . . A member of Company K captured some small pigs and roasted them whole. Two boys of Company I brought in a full-grown pig and slaughtered it in camp. . .

The Union diarist goes on to describe the brigade's marching to Moorefield on December 16 and then to

Lost River village where a "force of Confederates" was reported to be encamped. Although "the enemy had disappeared," the mission was a triumph:

> Concealed in the stable underneath some hay a comrade found 20 boxes of chewing tobacco. The Lynchburg plugs, a foot long, were highly prized, and deeper down in the hay something else was found that enlivened the visit to this benighted region of Lost River. It was two barrels of apple jack, known across the Delaware as 'Jersey Lightning.' The tobacco worked all right, and was soothing the men to sleep, but the officers had some difficulty preserving order an hour after the men found the apple jack. . .
>
> Quartermaster Hersh had captured half a dozen cattle. Two fat ones were slaughtered and the rest were taken along. . .
>
> On December 20 a fight was expected near Wardensville, a dozen miles ahead. . . The 87th went on double-quick and quick time, alternately, for two and one-half miles, but no enemy appeared in sight.
>
> The brigade halted for the night at Capon Springs, the noted summer resort at the foot of the Shenandoah mountains. Here the men slept in the beds of the large hotel . . . General Cluseret sent part of the regiment out to forage. They found some corn, flour and a few sacks of salt.

A story that has come down in Rudolph family tradition offers a clear picture of the military's priorities. Jacob Carr Rudolph, whose home was back of Hebron Church and who had enlisted in Company I, Eighteenth Virginia Cavalry, had been wounded. He managed to get back home and was in bed waiting for the wound to heal.

"The Yankees came through," Jack Rudolph tells the story now, "and learned about grandfather. He was an easy prisoner. The officer sent the sergeant into the house to get him, and the sergeant told grandfather to get out of bed and on his horse and come on. Grandfather sent Uncle Nathan out to get the horse. He saddled up the best horse they had. The commanding officer called in and asked what was taking so long, and the sergeant said the man was sick and it was taking him some time to get ready. The officer said 'We got too many sick to look after now; leave him alone and take his horse.' Grandfather got after Uncle Nathan for saddling up the best horse."

Jacob Rudolph, the wounded Confederate's namesake, recalls another piece of the story. "I heard from Aunt Polly Wertz that the Rudolph home place was located in a grove of sugar trees, and was so shaded that the sun never shone on the house; so they had tuberculosis and lung problems. But they made lots of maple sugar, which was the one thing of value they had left when the soldiers came through raiding and pillaging. They hid the sugar in a cupboard under the staircase, and the soldiers didn't find it."

Though this was nominally Union territory, people made no secret of their Confederate allegiance. When Jane and I were visiting ninety-year-old Marie Brill one afternoon in her home down near Hooks Mill—across the river from where the Timber Ridge camps are now—she brought out an envelope of much-used Confederate paper money, in denominations as small as 2½ cents, and two Confederate bonds in the amounts of $500 and $100. Dated August 19, 1861, the bonds promised interest payments every six months and return of the principal July 1, 1876. Only the first three interest coupons had been cut and cashed in.

"The bonds," Marie explained, "were bought by one

of the Klines, as I have been told, or by Captain Pugh. I think it was the Captain. He built this house we are sitting in, you know. About 1835. He was living here during the war."

Marie went on to tell some of the Captain Pugh stories that are part of valley legend. Born David Pugh in 1806 at Capon Bridge, he won his captaincy solely by virtue of his commanding presence. A member of the Virginia legislature in the early 1840s, Pugh was later a judge of the county court, then a delegate to the 1861 convention at Richmond which voted to secede from the Union. (If Marie is right that this vote was "over the Captain's vigorous protest," I am still more confused about Capon Valley political sentiments in the early 1860s.) Genealogist Maud Pugh reports that the Captain was "personally known to Henry Clay and Andrew Jackson [and was] a visitor at the White House during Jackson's presidency."

A wartime story passed down by Charlie Anderson has Captain Pugh and Samuel Davis going too far once in speaking their minds to a group of unwelcome blue-clad cavalrymen. The soldiers demanded that the cobbler and the captain take an oath of allegiance to the United States. When they refused, they were forced to ride with the raiders into Winchester, then in Union hands. Clapped in jail, the two intransigents held out for several weeks until, finding the food intolerable, they bargained to get their horses back, signed the oath, and came home. If the story has picked up something in over a hundred years of retelling, it still illustrates the tragicomic quality of war in this valley.

Another Davis family story is of the blue-uniformed lieutenant who spent the night as Maria and Samuel's unwelcome guest. The Union officer wakened in the morning to find his rifle missing, and didn't get it back until a threat to burn the barn led to the sudden discovery that the fickle firearm had gotten up during the night and wandered down into the corn field. When the fortunes of control shifted, the kitchen and dining room were full of gray-clad young men who were served a bountiful supper, bedded down for the night, then given a hot breakfast in the morning before they went on their way.

A more poignant war story is on two pieces of paper, apparently torn from a pocket diary or calendar, in cobbler Davis's ledger. One carries a letter written in an easily legible hand, not Samuel's:

> Dear Father:
> Being out of funds and barefoot, I have got Mr. Davis to make me a pair of boots and he has accommodated me by taking a note on you to the amount of thirty two dollars and a half ($32½) in bankable money. Please pay this and when I get paid off I will pay you back. I have been well but will go to the valley in a few days. I hope you are all well. I have not had a chance to write or hear from you for some time but expect I will have that pleasure in a few days. We will have some hard fighting in a few days but we will whip. I must now close. Please pay him as soon as you can send it by mail. The mail comes to Wardensville his post office address.
>
> > Your affectionate
> > Son

On the other sheet of paper is the note the boy wrote on his father:

H. Sr. Geo. Offut, dr.
   to Saml, Davis, Cr.
One pair of boots for Son
   $32.50
In bankable money.

With boots selling in 1864 at four or five dollars, this seems on its face to indict Samuel Davis as a war profiteer. But the boy's letter was apparently never sent to his father and there is no record of any payment ever being received. Another similar item in the ledger supports Mister Caudy's conjecture that young Offut was a Confederate soldier who had been wounded or had fallen sick and that the Davises had taken him in, perhaps because they knew his family. A Samuel and a John Offutt appear on constable Davis's list of creditors, and J.J.T. Offutt was both a practicing physician and the postmaster at Capon Bridge. The boy may have insisted on paying for his keep, and the Davises covered his pride.

It would be wrong to trivialize the most serious and critical passage in Yellow Spring history. The irony of ballot box stuffing that made Hampshire County technically part of the Union was heightened by subsequent years of local military maneuvers that yielded foot-long plugs of chewing tobacco and barrels of applejack. The stories that survive are characteristically about superficial aspects of war.

The sickening truth is written, of course, on the stones in the cemeteries at Hebron and Shiloh Methodist and Christian Church that are only a partial record of a bitterly high casualty rate for so small a community. The Confederate Monument in the Indian

Grove Cemetery at Romney, erected in 1867 as a declaration of continuing defiance, lists the names of 125 men who died defending slavery or states rights or whatever Confederacy stood for. The awful waste of it all is plainest when you drive along Winchester's Woodstock Lane, which divides 3,000 Confederate graves in the Stonewall Jackson Cemetery from half that many more Union stones in the National Cemetery. Most of the graves are marked "Unknown."

After the War

Willa Cather set her poignant and searing novel, *Sapphira and the Slave Girl*, in the area twelve miles northeast of Yellow Spring near Gore, Virginia where the author, born in 1873, had lived as a little girl. She includes in an autobiographical epilogue to *Sapphira* a report on the effects of the War Between the States on this area.

> After Lee's surrender, the country boys from Back Creek and Timber Ridge came home to their farms and set to work to reclaim their neglected fields. The land was still there, but few horses were left to work it with. In the movement of troops to and fro between Romney and Winchester, all the livestock had been carried away. Even the cocks and hens had been snapped up by the foragers.
> The Rebel soldiers who came back were tired, discouraged, but not humiliated or embittered by failure. The country people accepted the defeat of the Confederacy with dignity, as they accepted death when it came

to their families. Defeat was not new to those men. Almost every season brought defeat of some kind to the farming people. Their cornfields, planted by hand and cultivated with the hoe, were beaten down by hail, or the wheat was burned up by drought, or cholera broke out among the pigs. The soil was none too fertile, and the methods of farming were not very good. . . The boys still wore their army overcoats in winter, because they had no others, and they worked the fields in whatever rags were left of their uniforms.

The year the beloved novelist was born, George Davis, Samuel and Maria's son, and his bride, Hannah Spaid, moved into a new home that George had built 300 yards north of the original Davis place. Reports that have come down of George and Hannah's lives are the best starting place for filling in the Yellow Spring details of Willa Cather's sensitive description of the Reconstruction period.

George Davis is a legendary figure in Yellow Spring. Of medium height, he wore a beard that dropped halfway to his belt but flapped with his chin, which "meant considerable flapping," a grandson recalls, "for George was a man who spoke his mind regardless of who or where or what." Leaning forward in his saddle, with his beard jutting out ahead, "he always seemed to be getting there before the horse."

George had two religions. He drove or rode every Sunday evening and frequently at sundown during the week either to the Pentecostal Mission at Wardensville or to the meeting house the Pentecostals built up on the ridge, back of the Shiloh Methodist Church. "He didn't believe," ninety-four-year-old Benson LaFollette recalls, "in speaking in tongues. He said that if he couldn't understand what they were saying, he didn't think they did either." But he always led the praying, which sometimes went on longer than the sermon. "When he got wound up in his 'todays, tomorrows, and forevers,' the end of that beard would jump up and down a good foot. He seemed to be shaking it at the Lord and the Devil at the same time."

George's other devotion was to work, which he practiced, contrary to local standards, seven days a week. Spending the weekend in the blacksmith shop he had built down beside the road, near the river, he accommodated Hannah's protests about breaking the Sabbath by putting his left leg over the anvil to cut down the clanging.

At first most of his time went into farming. George raised hay and corn to take care of the animals, and enough wheat to provide flour for the family. His acre of buckwheat had a short growing season and would yield twenty bushels even from poor soil. It was ground on a homemade burr mill. George had chiseled out the ridges and grooves on the stones himself. His total cost for the mill was fifty cents for the axle.

"Fertilize" (a noun in Yellow Spring usage) for the fields came from the barnyard and chickenhouse, and phosphate from rocks on the mountain. A steep road climbed up Dug Hill to a lime kiln. Limestone rocks blasted out of the hillside were hauled on a narrow wagon with wide wheels to the kiln, cracked up into small pieces, and fired for eight to ten days until they became burnt lime powder.

George and his brothers kept up the tanning business their father had started. It was hard work. When a dozen or so hides, brought in to be worked "on halves," had accumulated, the men put them first on the fleshing ("flershing") table, half a maple log about six feet long and two feet in diameter. The round side was on top; four thick legs underneath brought it up to working height. Heavy fleshing knives were used to scrape the meat off the hides, which were then put to soak in a series of large wooden vats. After a brine that included ashes and lime had loosened the hair on the outside of the hides so it could be scraped off, the hides went into vats of tannic acid drawn from crushed chestnut-oak bark stripped from large trees across the river. The bark was more valuable than the lumber, the tree trunks often being left unused. The large spiked iron ball, which still lies today at the tannery site, was for grinding the bark; the power was drawn from a small stationary steam engine that also drove two rollers through which the hides were run before being hung on racks to dry.

The Davis shoemaking and leather-working operations declined sharply after the war as a consequence of increased competition. Cobbler John W. Spaid had the advantage, in addition to his skill, of being not only a Spaid but also by blood or marriage a LaFollette, a Brill, and a McKeever—which assured him a substantial family following. An even more formidable competitor, Flavius Josephus Sine, set up a leather shop at High View where he produced "Sine saddles" that became recognized as superior to all others. Among Samuel Davis's sons, only Julius remained interested in the shoemaking trade, and when the Spaid and Sine competition got too strong, he moved his business into Winchester.

George, born by family report with a "knack for making things," began spending more and more time at his forge. His son Caudy told me once, with obvious pride in his father's skills, the story about "a miller named

Schooler who lived over on North River. He broke five cogs, each about five inches high, on his mill drive shaft. He had a mechanic from Romney fix it . . . twice . . . but it didn't hold up. So he brought it to George Davis.

"My brother Tom and I worked the bellows and fed the fire for the forge. Father took out what was left of the old cogs and made new ones. Then he fastened them to the gear head with two rivets in each one. He made the rivets, too. When Schooler came back to get his drive shaft, he couldn't believe what he saw. 'How in the world did you do it?' he asked; and my father, boasting a little, answered, 'I can make anything to be made out of wood or iron.' Schooler repeated this to the mechanic in Romney who sent back word, 'Have him make himself a hornet's nest.' "

Knowing the value of his services, George charged for them accordingly. The going local rate for skilled work was seventy-five cents a day, a dollar at the outside. George asked and got $1.50. "I don't charge for doing the job," he told a customer who complained, "I charge for knowing how to do it."

His skill and ingenuity as the village blacksmith were also George Davis's credentials as its dentist. He could make forceps on his forge. Who could better use them than the maker? The artisan tail wagged the professional dog.

Forrest Davis recalls a story of his grandfather's professional solicitude. When he had finished pulling a tooth, George rewarded the patient with a large glass of well fortified red wine drawn from a straight-staved pine cask in the basement. If its color contributed to the client's confusion about what he was wiping from his lips, the strength of the dosage diminished his caring.

Depending on the blacksmith for oral surgery was one of the lesser nineteenth-century hazards to Yellow Spring health and physical well-being. There has never been a licensed doctor's office within eight miles of Yellow Spring and no hospital closer than Winchester or Romney. "Doc"—or "Setz"—Orndorff developed a reputation for medical understanding unsupported by any recorded or remembered credentials but testified to by the self-trained physician's saddlebag full of medicine bottles that his grandson Winthrop has preserved. Doc's daughter, Ida Mae Miller, who lived until she was ninety-nine, officiated at virtually every childbirth in the community. "She was one tough lady," a member of her flock recalls, "who could get all over you. But if she got there in time the baby's chances were a lot better."

If luck permitted, someone seriously ill could be gotten to a doctor at Capon Bridge or Winchester. John James Thornton Offutt (1826-1886) grew up at the Bridge, attended the medical college in Winchester, and returned to the valley to serve as both doctor and Capon Bridge postmaster during and after the war. His son, John Samuel Offutt (1864-1928), who received a thorough medical education, including "specialization in eye, ear, and throat" at Baltimore, probably at Johns Hopkins, became a giant in valley history. Never marrying, he is fabled for spending long weeks riding by horse and buggy up and down the valley, coming frequently to Yellow Spring, to provide whatever medical and surgical assistance was required.

For the most part, when a child was sick, or a sore opened, or a severe ache or pain set in, a worried mother drew on the resources at hand. We found in the house a copy of *The 20th Century Cook Book*, its print and condition confirming the title's suggestion that it was published at the turn of the century. An appendix includes "a table giving the remedial qualities of the common fruits and vegetables."

> Celery for any form of rheumatism and nervous dyspepsia. Lettuce for insomnia. Watercress for scurvy. Watermelon for epilepsy and for yellow fever. Blackberries for diarrhea.
>
> Onions are almost the best nervine known. Use for insomnia, for coughs and colds, and as a complexion curer. Eaten every other day they soon have a clearing and whitening effect on the complexion.

The cookbook also gives high marks to cranberries (for erysipelas, yellow or typhoid fever, some forms of dyspepsia, biliousness), pieplant (for purifying the blood and counteracting rheumatism), peanuts in soup form ("for strengthening, cleaning, healing, and nourishing"). All highly ripened fruits—sour oranges, lemons, figs, bananas, grapes, apples, and pineapples—are strongly recommended both for their general influence and for their specific virtues.

Although rheumatism was accepted as part of age's price, Maud Pugh reports another local procedure for fighting it: "Stop eating, live on milk for a week, bathe parts with alcohol camphor and vaseline. Don't use lemonade or other acid fruits. Quit coffee forever. Take Sal Hepatica until better."

The Yellow Spring materia medica depended largely on poultices, plasters, purges, patent medicines, and prayers. Poultices for young children were made of bread and milk. Those a little older were treated with a piece of slightly strong side meat, graduating with the years to goose grease fortified with pepper, mustard, or onion. "The stronger it is, the more it will draw"—or at least distract the mind from the inner affliction. Genealogist Pugh reports the recommended strategy when pneumonia threatened: "Use spray and make a big oily hot onion poultice, cover chest to keep poultice hot, go to bed, stay there until better; reheat or have a new poultice made if needed; use mild laxative."

Medicinal bitters were concocted by adding to alcohol, produced domestically, various camouflaging elements: sassafras, witch hazel leaves, dewberries, geraniums, sarsaparilla. If a purge seemed called for, it was compounded of bran, prunes, and sauerkraut juice. This reflected some softening of an earlier practice reported by historian Samuel Kercheval: "If a purge was used it was about half a pint of a strong concoction of walnut bark. This, when intended for a purge, was peeled downward; if for a vomit, it was peeled upward."

Warts were treated with castor oil, applied externally. Benson LaFollette tells of the juice from the brown jewel weed being used to cure poison ivy; others report a common reliance on homemade lye soap to stop the itch, "being careful to leave enough of the skin."

Patent medicines were big. Lydia Pinkham introduced her Vegetable Compound in 1875. Its unadvertised but critical ingredient was 21 percent alcohol. Dr. Hostetter raised the alcohol ante to 44 percent (88 proof) in his widely used Bitters. The bottles on the shelf beside my desk, gathered from locally auctioned boxes and contents, attest the attraction, perhaps the power, of the bottled placebo, heavily spiked and properly labeled: Healy & Bigelow's Kickapoo Indian

Cough Cure, Dr. Peter's Blood Vitalizer, Lung Balm (anonymous), Dr. Kilmer's Swamp Food, Pratt's Distemper and Pink Eye Cure (for equine disorders), Hamlin's Wizard Oil, Cremulsion for Coughs and Colds. My favorite, a gift from our friend Dorothy Bennett, is Seven Sutherland Sisters Hair Grower; their own tresses reached an advertised cumulative length of over thirty-five feet.

In an eight-page pamphlet, R.L. Wolcott of Brooklyn, New York, "Sole Proprietor of Pain Paint," offered not only health but wealth through "an exclusive deed of Agency, which will be sent to you on the purchase of a five-dollar package of Pain Paint powders... Mix them with seven pints of alcohol, add four gallons and three pints of water. This will fill about 336 two-ounce bottles, retailing for $84.00." Wolcott guaranteed ("I will not deceive you") that the Paint, applied to cheeks, temples, or head would cure toothache, neuralgia, headache, or catarrh; and that "diarrhea or dysentery will be quickly cured by wetting cloths in the remedy and applying them to the bowels."

Scoffing at medical procedures in Yellow Spring a century ago is too glib without comparing their effects with those of different miracle drugs in today's culture, George and Hannah Davis and their neighbors felt strongly, in any event, that "sending for the doctor every time you stub your toe means dying early."

We know much less of Hannah Davis than of George and have fewer details about women's role than men's in putting the valley back together after the war. Local folklore is restricted almost entirely to masculine personalities and exploits. Willa Cather, despite her own gender, wrote only of the problems the men faced. All

I ever got from Caudy Davis about his mother was that "she was a beautiful woman, inside and out."

In those years of travail, women's days were at least as long and as full as their husbands', their work in some ways harder, their talents and skills if anything greater. They came up short only on recognition.

Hannah had, with George's fleeting assistance, four children, several below par for the local course. Carson Brill appeared in 1875, Cora Jemima a year later, Thomas Boyd in 1880, Caudy George in 1886. They all lived into their eighties or nineties.

The best picture of women's place and lot in this chapter of valley history is in references scattered through Maud Pugh's *Capon Valley: It's Pioneers and Their Descendants*. (The spelling of "It's" is the author's.) She mentions, without complaint, the job description starting with carrying a new child almost every other year and delivering it painfully against odds that were, even with Ida Mae Miller's experienced midwifery, draining and frightening.

Ms. Pugh goes on to point out that this mass production was only the beginning. Feeding the family meant planting and hoeing a large garden; picking the produce; canning hundreds of quarts of beans, corn, peas, sauerkraut, apple sauce, and apple butter; and tending a wood fire. Dressing the family and keeping it warm started from carding wool, spinning thread or yarn, weaving the cloth; it went on to sewing most of the clothes and turning flour sacks and remnants of fabric into quilts. For Hannah Davis, the price of cleanliness was carrying water from the spring 150 feet away behind the tannery, or from the well, heating it on the wood stove, scrubbing each piece of clothing and bedding separately with soap she had made herself, wringing the pieces out by hand, and putting them on the line to dry regardless of temperature.

Physical labor was only part of the story. Although Hannah probably didn't object to sitting on the other side of the aisle from her husband in church, she must sometimes have winced at not owning anything; the land was George's and would of course go to their sons.

The sex caste system was deeply engraved. Early settler James Caudy, the legendary Indian fighter, had only one son, David, who died early. In his December 1, 1783 will, James left all of his land to David's three sons—and to each of his own three "beloved daughters, Ann Dulain, Margaret Wood, and Sarah Hancher . . . five shillings which I give to her and her heirs forever." Daniel Pugh's May 26, 1794 bequest to his "beloved wife, Sarah Pugh," was "300 pounds current money . . . but it is my will that she receive no part of said legacy until she has released her right to dower in and to my lands."

The situation didn't change much during the next hundred years. When Isaac Pennington died in 1894, his will left his farm near Yellow Spring to his son William, another, at Concord, to his sons John and Walter. Each of his three daughters—Lydia, Sarah, and Annie—received fifty dollars. Lydia, who became Marie Brill's mother, used part of her legacy to buy a sewing machine.

When I asked Marie how the women felt about all this she replied bluntly, "They didn't like it." Then she told the story of Lem (George and Maria's son) and Bertie Davis's abortive protest movement one Sunday morning at the Shiloh Methodist Church. "They were a spunky pair. Bertie was a Kelsoe. They lived just east of the Davis place. Bertie, who taught at Mt. Airy, was one of the prettiest and most popular girls around. I think their marriage [on August 24, 1884] was the first one in the new church that had just been built at Shiloh.

"Anyway, about a month later, they were there again for the regular Sabbath morning service. They walked a little way down the aisle, and sat down. Together. On the women's side."

Stopping and waiting to be asked what happened, Marie shook her head. "You know what happened. One of the men, Jonathan Brill the way I heard it from my mother, came over and tapped Lem on the shoulder, nodding toward Adam's side of the aisle. Lem got up and moved over."

Lemuel and Bertie Davis were more than a generation ahead of their time. Thirty years later, a referendum was held in West Virginia on an amendment to the state constitution to give women the right to vote. At a local estate sale I picked up copies of a flyer, published by the *West Virginia Patriot* and carrying the union bug, issued in connection with that referendum:

OPPOSE WOMEN SUFFRAGE

Because
> The men of the State are capable of conducting the government for the benefit of both men and women: their interests, generally speaking, being the same.

Because
> Women are not suffering from any injustice which giving them the Ballot would rectify.

Because
> The demand for the Ballot is made by a small minority of women, and the attempt of a minority to force its will upon the majority is contrary to the teachings of Democracy.

Because
> The Ballot in the hands of men has not proved a cure-all for existing evils and there is no reason to believe it would be more effectual in the hands of women. It has not been in the States where it exists.

Because
> Women now stand outside of politics, and having no political axe to grind, they are free to appeal to all parties to further good legislation in which they may be interested.

Because
> The basis of government is physical force. It isn't law but law enforcement, which protects society. Woman could not enforce the laws even if she made them.

Because
> Man's service to the State government is counterbalanced by woman's service in the Home. One service is just as essential to the welfare of the State as the other, but they can never be identical.

Vote NO on the Woman Suffrage Amendment.

The *Hampshire Review* for October 25, 1916 carried a news story reporting a speech that referred to a group of suffragettes as a "silk stocking poodle dog brigade, . . . an aggravation . . . represented by furs, feathers, and femininity." Two weeks later, on November 11, 1916, the *Review* reported the vote on the proposed amendment cast by the male residents of the county. Of the fifty-four votes cast at the Walnut Grove schoolhouse three were for the amendment, fifty-one against it. At the Mt. Airy polls, the vote was fifty-two to five to keep women in the kitchen.

There may have been another side to all of this. Our friend Elizabeth Frye points out that women could do what was demanded of them because in most homes "the extended family included old maid aunts, grandmothers, and daughters who were trained to work as soon as they were old enough to 'fetch and carry.' If you think in terms of the core family of today, life then seems impossible. The teenagers back then were taken out of school during heavy work times, unlike today's teenagers whose needs come first rather than the family's. In a way, the old families seem to have had more time and lived more leisurely than we do. Sunday was set aside for church and visiting."

The quilting bee is a stereotyped symbol of women's making pleasure of their assignments. Jane's collection of patchwork and friendship quilts, mostly from Hannah Davis's period, reflects both a human warmth and a strong sense of art. We have noted, though, a characteristic of the quilts that come up at local estate sales. Some are in the traditional patterns: Log Cabin, Turkey Tracks, Flower Garden, Star, Nine Patch, Double Wedding Ring, and the others. Yet few of them would be considered classics of stitchery; where fine quilters put twelve or even fourteen stitches to the inch, most of the Yellow Spring cotton quilts have seven or eight. A good many are of homespun wool, recycled pieces from old dresses or skirts; and instead of being stitched they are tied with little knots of yarn. Hannah and her neighbors may have felt less the enchantment of art than the pressures of approaching winter.

Finding quilting bees a "narrowing of women's minds into needlework and social entertainment," Maud Pugh goes on: "Girls, it was thought, did not . . . need an education since the husband would do the 'writing and figuring' for the household; so a girl must marry. She had no other alternative. Her father left the sons most of the property. No doors of livelihood were open to her; but the most pitiable phase of the situation is that she had no choice even in marriage. She must wait to be chosen."

Like other early American outposts, this was a man's valley. The majority (that is, masculine) view was that "woman's service was in the home"—to be taken largely for granted.

Yet the largest breakthrough, perhaps in all of the valley's history, came immediately after the war in an area that was considered women's business. I mentioned earlier Lottie Kline's recalling that Maria Davis "gave her children all the education they ever got. It took with the girls but not with the boys." George was one of those boys. Strong on fundamentalist religion, he didn't, by one of his son's accounts, "put much stock in education."

So it was probably at Hannah's urging, while she was carrying her first child, that George donated a thousand square feet of land fifty yards north of the house to the county. In 1875 this became the site for the Walnut Grove School.

Building the one-room structure was a community affair. The studs and siding were sawed on site with what was literally one-horse-power equipment. Walk-

Washington, the surveyor, and his sketch of Lost River
encountering Sandy Ridge (Library of Congress)

Hebron Lutheran Church (1848–   )
(Courtesy Ruth Ryan Rudolph)

The Mountain House,
Capon Springs
About 1900

The old Davis place at middle age, about 1900
(Courtesy Forrest and Willetta Davis)

The Davis Tannery after it
had been abandoned

BELOW: Tilbury Orndorff with friends outside his stillhouse (about 1925) and
RIGHT: Tilbury in retirement.
(Genevieve Watson and Norman Walker Collections)

ABOVE: Rail bus No. 11, Winchester and Western Railroad, picking up passengers at Capon Lake Inn, 1923.
(L.P. Winnemore Collection, courtesy Samuel Davis)

RIGHT: John Kline in 1923
(Genevieve Watson Collection)

Benson La Follette
LEFT: seated with friend, 1917
RIGHT: 1984

Abigail Miller Kline and Ida Mae Orndorff
Miller making apple butter.
(Genevieve Watson Collection)

Monument to Henry
and Juliah Kump in
family graveyard.
(Photograph by James
Megronigle)

Yellow Spring store, about 1910
(Genevieve Watson Collection)

George Franklin Davis
1848–1927

Hannah Spaid Davis
1849–1914

George and Hannah (CENTER) with Carson, Cora, Thomas, and
Caudy in front of Davis Place II, 1890's

(Above photographs from the Etta and Franklin Davis Collection)

Caudy George Davis
Ada Spaid Davis
Married June 6, 1912

1980

About 1960

(Sybil Davis Forrester Collection)

LEFT: Coming up to the lane to Tannery, 1984
(Photo by Howard Lichtenstein)

RIGHT: Looking across the river, which is just below the first trees
(Photo by Howard Lichtenstein)

Looking south
(Photo by James Megronigle)

ing slowly around in a circle at the end of a twelve-foot shaft, the horse turned a wheel geared to a vertical saw; a ratchet moved the log or plank forward. The rafters were hewn with axes, the boards planed by hand. George forged the nails in his shop.

Completing the building, the men went on to build the teacher's desk at the end opposite the door. Benches in front of the desk were for the smallest children, those at the side for third to sixth graders. One more bench at the back was enough for students staying on into the seventh and eighth grades. The only out-of-pocket cost was for the stove in the center of the room and for its pipe going up through the roof (a perennial and legendary fire hazard).

Important as the Walnut Grove School was for Hannah's and the neighbors' children, its building was equally significant as a reflection of the valley's breaking out of a century's bondage. The mountain people deeply resented the tidewater-Virginia practice of denying, in practical effect, any significant public education to children born west of the Blue Ridge. As early as 1863, when the fighting was still at its height, the new West Virginia legislature adopted a public education policy. Virtually unfunded, the enactment was little more at first than a statement of intent. Yet as soon as the war was over, and while they were still destitute, people across the state began implementing that purpose. In a fifteen-year period, from the late 1860s to the early 1880s, four other new schools in addition to Walnut Grove were built in the Yellow Spring area: first Ell Ridge, back of Concord, and Mt. Airy, just across the river and above Loman's Branch; then Red Bud on Back Creek, and Willow Chapel at Watson Town (now Capon Springs).

This rebirth of education was so dramatic that it would be easy to exaggerate its immediate effects. The continuing shortage of funds meant relying for teachers on local men and women whose only qualifications were that they had themselves finished the eight grades and were willing to work for a pittance. Parents sent their children to whichever school they preferred and the teachers' compensation depended, at least as a practical matter, on the enrollment. Moving around from school to school, the teachers' usual tenure was two to three years. With attendance entirely voluntary and progress from one grade to another automatic, both discipline and motivation were serious problems.

The report cards that Philip and Bertie Creswell brought home in 1875 from the Riverdale School at Hooks Mill, one of the few established before the war, provide insights into both curricular and grading practices. Philip was in seventh grade, Bertie in sixth. Teacher John Tompkins recorded their performance in Orthography (Spelling), Reading, Writing, Diction, Arithmetic, Grammar, and Geography, reporting too on their Progress, Deportment, and Application. The evaluation was on the basis of each student's position in a particular grade. The impressiveness of Philip's bringing home six firsts and a second and Bertie's mostly seconds and thirds, was diminished by the realization that with twenty students registered at Riverdale that year the number in each class averaged between two and three. Both children's Progress was recorded as "Rapid" and their Deportment as "Good." Bertie was credited with "Very Assiduous" Application.

The necessary dependence on untrained teachers meant that the educational level rose only slowly above its source—except for the infusion that resulted from the arrival in the valley in the early 1870s of an extraordinary man who survives in local legend only as Professor Throop. Identified as a graduate of Harvard, Throop taught at the Old Kedron schoolhouse at Capon Bridge, where he also conducted a "normal school" to which other teachers came for training. Throop had two consuming loves in life. If his dedication to teaching made him the unofficial dean of valley education, his effectiveness was regrettably diminished by an equal liking for what his colleague Maud Pugh refers to compassionately as "the forbidden juice." Mixing his books and his bourbon in a manner his students were inclined to indulge without criticism, he eventually drowned his remarkable pedagogical talents.

It would be wrong to suggest that an educational renaissance occurred overnight in the valley or to disregard the limitations the early teachers faced. It took a long time for education to make up what it had lost during the hundred years before the Civil War. Fifty years later the elementary school budget for the Capon District still authorized employing teachers for only six months a year, at thirty to fifty dollars a month. The catching-up process remains incomplete even today.

It would be an equal mistake to minimize the part these teachers played in bringing dawn to that hundred years of darkness. Within twenty years after the war, par for going to school was raised in the valley from about zero to eight years. Although the Mt. Airy and Ell Ridge schoolhouses are today in the final stages of dilapidation, Walnut Grove stands, well preserved, as a monument to a band of early teachers who did the best they could.

After summarizing the story of destitution and heartache that were the immediate aftermath of war, Willa Cather reports another, new dimension that was added to life in the valley as it was gradually restored to livable quality:

> This new generation was gayer and more carefree than their forebears, perhaps because they had fewer traditions to live up to. . . . The young couples were poor and extravagant and jolly. They were much given to picnics and camp meetings in summer, sleighing parties and dancing parties in the winter. . . .

Religion's exacting dictates were redefined in more tolerant terms. If the central tradition continued to be Work, larger opportunities were included for recreation of one kind or another.

Hunting and fishing topped the list for the men and boys, serving the interests of both sport and table. This has always been great deer country, and the mountainside also yielded bear, red and brown fox, coons, and an occasional panther to liven things up. Squirrel or rabbit or quail pie were more staples than delicacies, and the Thanksgiving turkey was wild and fresh.

The best fishing came from gigging on the river during the winter. After a slot had been cut through the ice, two or three giggers would wait there while the others moved toward the slot, tapping the surface to encourage the fish toward the opening. The sharp three-pronged hand-forged gigs, mounted on long poles, had to be driven with practiced eye and timing to impale the bass or trout or crappies, two-or-three-or-five pounders, in the middle of the back.

"Tournament riding" was a more spectacular diversion, although its medieval and royal antecedents make it hard to fit into an Appalachian context. The popularity of the sport probably went back to so many young men's wartime cavalry experience. Its annual revival on Heritage Weekend at Moorefield, in neighboring Hardy County, still brings it to life.

A hundred-yard straightaway passes three posts about fifteen feet high from which arms at the top reach out over the course. Flexible holders suspended from the arms hold small white celluloid rings loosely in place.

The master of ceremonies in the judge's stand rises at the appointed hour to announce the proceedings in Elizabethan-Appalachian prose and accent. At a trumpet sound, the tournament master announces the first rider and calls him to the head of the course. "Sir Arthur Godlove of Sandy Ridge. Approach Sir Knight."

The contestant carries a ten-foot lance. At the command "Ride, Sir Knight," he stands in his stirrups, bends forward at the waist, puts his horse at full gallop down the course, and tries to pick off with his lance the white ring suspended at each post. Returning to the judges with three rings on his lance gives Sir Arthur a perfect score for the round. The other riders are then called in turn.

The rings used for the first run are two inches in diameter. The three-ring survivors go to a second round, with inch-and-a-half rings. If there are still ties to be run off, one-inch rings are placed in the holders for a third go at them. A longer blast of trumpetry accompanies the tournament winner's approach to the stand, where he is saluted fittingly for threading needles at full gallop.

A hundred years ago, the climax of the tournament

riding season was the annual fall pageant at the Mountain House at Capon Springs. Ten to fifteen of the best riders in the valley were invited to compete. Announcements were issued with heraldic flourish and the course, laid out along the road below the creek, was trimmed with bunting and banners. Hundreds of local people mixed at the pageant with guests from the hotel, some of whom had bid against each other to establish a winner's purse; the successful bidder's daughter was named Queen of the Pageant.

The Kump brothers won the tournament for several years running in the 1890s. Kerr Kump later credited the purses, sometimes substantial, for paying the college expenses that led him to the state legislature and his brother to the West Virginia governorship.

But tournament riding was a sport of kings in which only a few could qualify. The most satisfying postwar Yellow Spring diversion was music, which offered the twin advantages of being cheap and being best enjoyed when people made it together. Singing was free, and a guitar or fiddle or melodeon was easily come by.

Caudy Davis, George and Hannah's youngest son, recalled, when he was ninety-six, most of the band his brothers Carson and Tom had put together. "Ed Kelsoe was on cornet, Sprig Orndorff on baritone, and Til Heishman on trombone. Tom played alto and Carson bass. I was just a grasshopper and they put me on the drums. But when I was about ten, Carson bought me a fiddle and Will Lupton, who worked for us, taught me how to play it." Either the Davis pickup group or the Mt. Airy School band performed at community picnics, church socials, and family reunions.

At a more professional level, Yellow Spring had its own nationally recognized music man. Professor Jesse

B. Aikin was living here in 1876, when he published *Imperial Harmony: A Choice Collection of Sacred Music (in Aikin's Character Notes)*. He had autographed the copy I found in a box-and-contents at an estate sale and now have on my desk.

Aikin was no ordinary musician. He tried to "simplify the labor of learning to read musick" by printing the tones of the scale in different shapes—a variety of round, oval, square, and triangular forms—"which the singer learns to read at a glance." The music in the 1876 collection is printed in these "Aikin Character Notes." Despite the publishers' expression of unrestrained confidence that they were initiating a revolution in musical communication, the Yellow Spring professor's (credentials unidentified) system didn't catch on, and his work is now forgotten—except that he also invented and patented the device that permits an organ keyboard to be transposed into various keys. The full Aikin story remains to be uncovered and told.

Aikin's collection of hymns is a reminder that although the second half of the nineteenth century produced little classical music in America, it was a golden age for songs. The hymn-writers took the lead: one of them, Lowell Mason, wrote over 1,200 ("From Greenland's Icy Mountains" and "Nearer My God to Thee"). At first, the three-or-four-voice choirs at the churches took their pitch from a tuning fork; after the opening verse the congregation joined in. Organs came in some time after the war.

One of the best-known national names in the Yellow Spring area during this period was Stephen Collins Foster, whose more than 400 songs were written between 1840 and 1860. When everybody got together for hoe-downs, square dances, and singings, the area's fid-

dlers also drew for their repertoire on the thousands
of popular songs that came from the minstrel shows
produced by white men with soot on their faces. James
A. Bland wrote over 700 minstrel songs ("Carry Me
Back to Old Virginny," "In the Evening By the Moon-
light," "Dem Golden Slippers," which sold over 100,000
copies) but never took visible part in the productions.
He wasn't permitted to—because he was black. So was
Scott Joplin, whose "Maple Leaf Rag" introduced
America to ragtime in 1896.

The big social event of the year was the "pelsering."
The word isn't in the dictionary and nobody is willing
to vouch for its spelling. The custom was like the "bels-
nichling" which the German settlers in the valley had
brought with them a century earlier, and I have also
come across references to a similar custom called
"Christlinking."

For a week or two in mid-and late December, pelsering parties circulated after dark through the neighborhood. Masked and costumed, with simulated hunched
backs or other deformities, the pelserers spoke in
strange accents. You let them in when they came to
the door, watched their antics, then tried to pierce their
disguises. Specially prepared candies and cookies were
part of the custom.

The pelsering tradition continued to play a large part
in Yellow Spring pleasures until the 1930s. One of
George and Hannah's grandsons, Frank Davis, attributes its disappearance to a development one night
when he was ten or twelve. It was discovered that the
pelserers performing in the Davis living room were
actually covering for collaborators who were down at
the barn stealing the coils out of the Model T. Frank
recalls taking down the shotgun, putting in a twelve-

gauge shell, and firing it toward the barn. "I meant to shoot way over their heads. But when I found the shot in the wall the next morning I realized that I hadn't missed them by more than a few inches. There was never much pelsering around here after that." A less dramatic theory is that pelsering became part of a custom that spread across the country, that the pranking started a little earlier each year, and that it eventually turned into Halloween.

We have upstairs, in our granddaughters' room, two sentinels of Christmas past, probably from those years after the war. The little wooden wheelbarrow, ten inches high and about twice that long, is carefully made, to exact scale and in perfect working condition. The hobby horse, hand-carved, brightly painted and fully equipped with leather saddle and stirrups and halter, waits for a two-year old to climb on its back. The toys speak quietly of the labor and love that went into Christmas when there wasn't a penny to spare for extras.

I see in my imagination a Sunday in mid-or late February, 1888. George and Hannah Davis have come with their four children across the field and past the tannery to the house here. Patriarch Samuel, now seventy-seven, has been tiring rapidly and Maria has arranged for everybody's getting together once more. Eight of their twelve sons and daughters are still living, six of them close enough by to come for the day.

Samuel never really recovered from the war. A few months after Lee's surrender at Appomattox, an epidemic took two of the younger children. Having lost his livestock to the Union foragers, Samuel found himself so hard put financially that in 1870 it took pressure from the constable's office he had once held to enforce a payment of $152.50 on his thirty-one-year-old "land purchase note due the estate of Joel Ellis." Son Walter's tragic death, a month before the gathering, has brought the pangs of final defeat. It is hard for his sons and daughters to change an old man's feeling that things haven't worked out the way they should have.

Later in the evening, after the others have left, Maria sits beside Samuel's bed to talk a little more. He says something again about it all having been hard work and about how much of that work the war undid. Maria listens quietly, perhaps thinking to herself that her work has been just as hard and that war is one of men's poorer ideas. But then she does her own reviewing of their forty-four years. Ten children raised to maturity, eight still living and doing all right. Five schools in the neighborhood now where there were none before. Dozens of neighbors, close friends, instead of the handful of settlers they first knew. She sums it up: "Sam, you and I came to a lonely wilderness. We have done our part in building a family and a community."

Samuel Davis was buried at Hebron. The inscription on the large tombstone in the middle of the older part of the cemetery says more of the custom of the times than of his distinguishing character:

> Samuel Davis
> Born May 19, 1811
> Died March 6, 1888.
> A precious one from us has gone
> A voice we loved is stilled
> A place is vacant in our hearts
> Which never can be filled.

Maria lived for another twenty years and then was buried beside her husband, with a simpler inscription: "Nearer my God to Thee/Nearer to Thee." They remain the presiding spirits at what we now call Tannery, but what will always be the old Davis place.

Mountain Spirits

In all our years here, I have never met a still. This doesn't mean there aren't some around. The lonesome bottles on the shelves of the small state liquor store in Wardensville mock any belief that they constitute the sole source of local supply. Jack Gentry, our longtime close friend and fellow weekend traveler from Washington, sometimes gave us for Christmas a bottle, lacking either label or revenue stamps, that confirmed his better acquaintance than mine with certain aspects of local enterprise. I still nurture one of the two flasks, marked simply "Peach Brandy/1938," that our neighbor Bill Massey left when he and Mary moved to Hawaii.

Such limited personal exposure confines me to putting this spiritual subject in historical perspective.

Home brewing and moonshining were clearly native crafts in the valley, cabin industries that probably reached their fullest perfection in the late nineteenth century. Their rudiments were either inherited or very early acquired common knowledge. Caudy Davis, George and Hannah's youngest son, recalled with satisfaction his youthful partnership with his brother Tom, sometime during the 1890s, in brewing up a batch of Old Hen.

Grinding up some rye grain when their father was away on one of his Pentecostal evenings, the juvenile offenders put it in a five-gallon crock, added sugar and yeast, filled the crock with water, and let it set down behind the pigsty. As it fermented during the next week, a layer of froth came to the top, stayed there for several days, and then settled back down. The brew was ripe.

The next Sunday, Tom and Caudy begged off from church so they could take care of their product. Straining the brew and putting it in bottles, they dumped the tired grain beside the feed trough, counting on the hogs to destroy the evidence, which they did.

"When the family got home," Mister Caudy told the story, "Father happened to go back to look at the hogs. There were three of them. One was lying on his belly, all four legs pointing in different directions. One was on his haunches, front legs stiff. The sow was flat on her back, all four feet sticking straight up. That Old Hen was potent beer."

Mister Caudy couldn't remember what view his father took of the sacrilegious enterprise. The family recollection is that George Davis considered beer and wine proper rewards for a day's hard labor, or for suffering an extracted molar, but that he drew a sharp line between lower and higher proof beverage.

The Hampshire Review for October 11, 1888 carried two Yellow Spring items. One was in the official report of the recent County Court session:

> License were ordered to be issued to Tilberry Orondoff
> to retail spirituous liquor at his distillery at Yellow
> Springs.

In the next column was a "Public Notice."

> I desire to inform the public that I now have license to
> retail whiskey and am prepared to furnish it in quan-
> tities of five gallons or less. I do my own manufacturing
> and keep nothing but pure rye whiskey. T. Orndorff.
> Yellow Springs, W. Va.

This remarkable desire to seek official endorsement
for an activity most of his neighbors handled infor-
mally made it seem worthwhile to look further into T.
Orndorff's story. The help of his great-grandson Norman Walker has rewarded the adventure.

The initial T, it turns out, was for Tilbury, rather
than Tilberry; his writing, about par for the local
course, led to a lifetime's confusion of his name. The
Orndorffs (pronounced without the second "r") had
come to the valley early in the century. The David
Orndorff who was one of cobbler Samuel Davis's first
customers, was Tilbury's father or grandfather.

Born on October 8, 1845, Tilbury was only seventeen
when he enlisted, in August of 1862, in Company D of
the First Regiment of the Virginia Partisan Rangers,
part of the Sixty-Second Mounted Infantry. Transferred to Company I of the Eighteenth Virginia Cavalry, he engaged in a year's fighting before being
captured at the Battle of Winchester on January 2,
1864. During the next eighteen months he was shuttled
between Union prison camps at Wheeling, Camp
Chase, and Fort Delaware.

After Appomattox, Tilbury was offered his liberty in
exchange for an oath of allegiance to the Union. His

June 20, 1865 application for the oath describes him: "Height 5'9"; complexion Light; hair also Light; eyes Blue."

Returning to his home in the valley, up toward Wardensville, Tilbury set about putting the family farm back in shape. His marriage to Amanda McKeever united the Orndorffs with another long line of valley veterans. It was a formal wedding. (His great-grandson owns and puts on with pride the long black coat, trousers, and vest that Tilbury wore that day.)

Time has erased the circumstances that constrained Tilbury to take up with the county court what was usually considered a private matter. Although the possibilities include ambition and nobility of character, his great-grandson's conjecture is that the forty-three-year-old farmer had had some previous experience that led to official questioning of his amateur status and that he took out a license as a form of plea bargaining.

In this connection Norman reports the mountain moonshiner's stock response when the "revenuers" uncovered his still. "All right. No license. Couldn't afford it. Lock me up. But you'll have to arrange for somebody to take care of the wife and kids. I'm all they've got. And I'd be obliged if you'd not do too much damage to the cooker and the coil." Which was often enough to remind the sheriff or constable, who lived just down the road and went to the same church, of some other more serious criminal activity that required attention.

Thanks to Barbara Harr's (another of Tilbury's descendants) regard for history, his recipe for making mash was preserved in its original longhand form and was recently rediscovered. Reportedly developed first by his father Jonah, it obviously predates Tilbury's public pronouncement that he kept "nothing but pure rye whiskey."

To make Corn and Rye.

To make 60 gals. mash. Put in mash tub 5½ gals water at a temperature of 170° or 180°. Stir in 30# corn meal so as to be free from lumps, let stand 15 mins. Add boiling water till temperature is raised to 190°, cover and let stand 1½ hours. Then stir till cooled to 120°. Add 50 gals cold water and add yeast, stir well. Will be ready for use in 72 hours.

Given by T. Orndorff

The discovery and circulation of the Orndorff recipe has led to considerable speculation. That the recipe calls for neither sugar nor malt violates conventional local experience and the commonly understood chemistry of spiritous endeavor; for malt helps convert the starch in grain into sugar, from which the alcohol is derived. The recipe Tilbury got from his father, which probably reflected the high cost of sugar and malt, would have produced a discouragingly low alcoholic content. By the time Tilbury went into commercial production he was almost certainly using malt (a pound or two) and about thirty pounds of sugar in his sixty-gallon brew.

Although local recollection is confused about this, Tilbury's stillhouse was probably back of the mill and behind what was then Asie Cline's home and is now the Watson place. He probably used a pot still, made of tin and constructed of lower and upper parts that were pasted together with a flour-and-water dough so that if the fire got too hot the upper part would lift off without wrecking the whole still. The top of the cooker narrowed to a five-inch-or-so cap that led off through a tapered arm to the worm, a coil of copper pipe running down through a barrel of cold water to a nozzle at the bottom.

Brewing up a sixty-gallon batch of rye mash, Tilbury poured it when it was ripe into the cooker, being careful to leave the "slops" in the barrel. Four or five hours of cooking at about 170 degrees Fahrenheit (where alcohol boils but water doesn't) gave him ten gallons or so of "sweet mash singlings," which he then cooked again to produce seven or eight gallons of 100-proof "doublings." Filtering the semiprecious liquid through some charcoal yielded the "pure rye whiskey" Tilbury had advertised for sale.

In the meantime, the honest distiller added some more ground grain, malt, and sugar to the slops, filling the barrel again with water. Repeating the fermentation and cooking processes produced another run, this time of "sour mash" whiskey that appealed particularly to local taste.

At other times, Tilbury started with fruit instead of grain: apples that had been pressed and the cider left until it started to turn, or cut-up peach halves that had been covered with water and left to ferment. Then the brew went into the cooker. Brandy was trickier than whiskey, depending on a skillful balance of fruit and sugar content, adding raisins to hurry the process but not too much, and other techniques that artists in residence kept secret. Good brandy—white lightning—sold for two or three times as much as whiskey. Tilbury wouldn't have stooped to the practice of producing a fake brandy by letting apple cores or peaches sit in a crock of corn liquor until it took on their taste.

A distiller of such uncommon quality would also have held off the market, except when it was unusually active, several runs of whiskey to be stored in two or three barrels kept in the dirt basement under his house. Made of tight coopered white oak and charred inside, these barrels held their contents indefinitely. A year's aging, preferably three or four, produced a premium product that brought a substantially higher price.

The barrels Tilbury used represented another of the valley's important but less publicized natural resources. The August 1985 issue of *Wonderful West Virginia* eulogizes "the White Oak . . . King of West Virginia's Forests," which has the unique quality, in technical terms, that "the small vessels, the conducting arteries of the living tree become blocked with transverse structures called tyloses" which isn't true of other timber, even of red and black oak. To Tilbury Orndorff this meant, more simply, that the white oak barrels didn't leak. Coopering was an active local enterprise. Hundreds of these barrels were floated on rafts down the Monongahela, Kanawha, Ohio and Mississippi rivers to New Orleans and then shipped to Europe. The white oak was also prized as a superior construction material for blockhouses, forts, bridges, and the planking on sailing vessels. When we walked through the trees across the river recently, looking for gypsy moth egg cases, Rick Smith, from Camp Rim Rock, who knows and loves wood, pointed with special admiration to the white oaks we came to. There aren't many left.

Distiller Orndorff might have felt some concern, probably not much, about pressure that was developing in opposition to his chosen profession. The Prohibitionist Party had been organized in 1867, and in the 1880s the *Hampshire Review* had added "Temperance" to the masthead's statement of principles the editors endorsed. The October 11, 1888 issue of the newspaper,

which carried T. Orndorff's advertisement, also set out
official notice of the state legislature's adoption on February 17, 1887 of Joint Resolution No. 16. Two-thirds
of the members of both houses had voted to recommend
an amendment to the West Virginia Constitution providing that "the manufacture, sale and keeping for
sale, of all intoxicating liquors, mixtures and preparations . . . are forever prohibited in this State. . . ."

Neither the newspaper editors nor the legislators
were very serious. The *Review*'s largest advertisers
were the commercial distilleries and the purveyors of
high-proof patent medicines. In its next issue, a full
column was devoted to reprinting a speech supporting
the "fundamental principle of free government" made
before the United Anti-Prohibition Club in Texas. The
West Virginia senators and assemblymen also managed to carry water on one shoulder and "intoxicating
liquors, mixtures and preparations" on the other for
the next twenty-seven years.

West Virginia "went dry" in 1914. The *Review* reported in its March 31, 1915 issue that during the six
"dry months" ending February 28th of that year arrests
for drunkenness in Hampshire County dropped to 203,
compared with 737 during the comparable six "wet
months" a year earlier—resulting in a saving of 28,585
work-house prisoner meals. Perhaps so, although I
wonder some about whether, at least here in the valley,
the relationship between supply and demand and the
consequences in terms of excessive usage were affected
that much by the changing letter of the law.

It would be wrong to minimize the mischief that
high-proof products played in postwar Capon Valley
history. Yellow Spring folklore includes its quota of

stories of men who devoted a lopsided share of their later lives to embalming the military frustrations of their youth.

Lem Cline, Asie's brother, who lived across the river from the Davises, is one of those who emerge in these recountings in larger than life-size proportions. One of his grandsons recalls Lem's frequent river crossings in the evening, on his way home from the stillhouse where he had spent an hour or so swapping war stories and sampling veteran Tilbury's current endeavor. Setting out boldly in his rowboat from the western shore, Lem, standing upright but with difficulty in the stern, invariably toppled overboard in midstream, protesting the hail of bullets he felt pouring down on him from the ghostly Feds still holding the bluff that rises from the eastern bank.

Lem's homeward path also led across the neighboring Davis property, and Carson, George and Hannah's oldest son, told his children of his boyhood terror one evening when he was working that part of his father's field. Lem, carrying a jug under one arm and a gun under the other, got momentarily confused about the boundary line and started threatening the neighbor boy with trespass, to be punished on the spot—until the befuddled enforcer toppled, in temporary peaceful oblivion, from the fence he was climbing to get at Carson.

While these stories, embroidered with a century of yarn spinning, probably do Lem Cline a measure of injustice (which just as probably he wouldn't object to), they reflect, even if in distortion, the price that went with exploiting one of the valley's natural resources. Easily produced from raw materials as close at hand as the nearest grain field and the orchard behind the house, and costing little more than some semiskilled labor, whiskey and brandy were part of the Yellow Spring economy, principal ingredients in many of its medications, and also staples in some people's regular diets.

On balance, though, John Barleycorn's influence on local history has been grossly exaggerated. Liking their liquor about as much as a lot of other people, the mountaineers hated taxes more. The distinguishing Appalachian characteristic was less an excessive use of alcohol than a stubborn contempt for legal technicalities regarding its production. Moonshining was traditionally part of a broader do-it-yourself, make-it-yourself way of life that included a strong feeling against having to pay taxes for the doing and making, especially when you didn't have the money to buy the product or pay the taxes. History's grand jury would indict a good many of Yellow Spring's leading citizens for unlicensed manufacture, but only about the national average for conspicuous consumption.

The More Slowly Things
Change . . .

A new century found Yellow Spring, West Virginia still a long way from anyplace else, tending to its own affairs. People came in or went out, by foot or horse, when they had to. On busy days the post office handled ten or twelve pieces of mail, most of it local. The county seat was a hard day's travel over the mountains, the state house at Charleston a place only heard about, Washington a foreign capital. At election time, candidates for national office carried or lost the valley precincts by riding the local sheriffs' coattails.

This all changed more in the next few years than in the previous hundred, principally for two reasons. One was a war, set on a world stage; people whose families had lived for a century-and-a-half in virtual isolation became for the first time fully committed participants in a nation's undertaking. More importantly, the way of life this remoteness had molded came under the influence of strangers called Science and Technology.

On March 17, 1917, a Sunday afternoon, thirty men and women gathered at the Walnut Grove schoolhouse to organize what they decided to call the Young People's Union Christian Endeavor League. A resolution adopted at the close of the meeting provided "that this organization will meet promptly at 2:30 p.m. each Sabbath." Which it did. But only three times.

S. R. Brill was elected president of the new league, Vause Whitaker vice-president, Madison B. Kline treasurer. The secretary's duties were assigned to Jefferson Davis with his wife being named assistant secretary—probably because Jeff wanted Angie to do the writing. Office holding was still a male prerogative in Yellow Spring, 1917.

Although the recorded minutes of the three meetings are brief, they reflect the convenors' intent. Some of those at the gathering had attended services that morning at Timber Ridge Christian, others at Shiloh Methodist or at Hebron Lutheran. They recognized that sectarianism's walls had crumbled under the pressure of marriages across denominational lines; it was time for ecclesiastical "union". And if weekly devotionals were scheduled for Sabbath afternoons, young people who showed signs of backsliding might find them more convenient than early morning Sunday school.

At that first meeting, the group selected, with unconscious irony, the Scripture lesson for the following Sabbath: Exodus 20:3-18 and Matt. 6:9-11—the Commandments and part of the Lord's prayer. The irony is in the verse from Exodus 20:6—"Thou shalt not kill." For on Monday, April 2, 1917, the day after the third meeting of the Young People's Union Christian Endeavor League, President Wilson advised Congress that the country must declare war against Germany. This was done two days later. Christian endeavor, especially by young men, had to be turned from ploughshares to swords. The Walnut Grove sessions were never reconvened.

Available records indicate that twenty-seven men went off to war from Yellow Spring, Concord, Lehew, High View, and Capon Springs. Four enlisted voluntarily, all in the Navy. Sidney Carrier and Ernest and Harry Anderson were on convoy duty throughout the war. Ashby Mason, who had taught at Walnut Grove and Ell Ridge, was assigned to office duty in Washington.

The first draft call in Hampshire County was in August of 1917. The quota was 104, and Lucian Wilson and Charles Frank were on that early list.

Ross Cline, Charles Peacemaker, and Albert and Boyd Simmons were among the fifty-four inductees who left Romney by special train on May 27, 1918 for Camp Lee. A scheduled sendoff was canceled by J. W. Shull, County Health Officer, because "a large gathering might be the cause of the spread of the influenza epidemic." Ten days later, Cleal Miller, Nelson Mason, and William Himelwright were in another larger contingent of 114 ("all white," the *Hampshire Review* noted, "except two") that entrained at Romney for Camp Lee. An early June call took Walton Brill, Ernest Cline, Lohr LaFollette, Herman and Carter Racey, Franklin Spaid, and Luther Stine.

Ninety-four-year old Benson LaFollette, Yellow Spring's only surviving veteran, recalls experiences that were typical. He was inducted in late June of 1918, along with Arthur Nelson, Charles Mason, Harry and

John Larrick, Irvan Kump, Loring Miller, and thirty
others from Hampshire County. The *Review* reports:
"On Friday afternoon [June 27th] a large crowd assem-
bled [at the railroad station in Romney] to honor the
Hampshire boys who left that evening for Camp Lee."
W. F. Wingman, president of the Hampshire County
Red Cross Society, presided at the speechmaking,
which was mostly about buying Liberty Bonds. "Com-
fort kits and lunch boxes were distributed to the de-
parting soldiers, after which they left on a special train
at 6:40 o'clock." A band played "Over There" as the
train pulled out.

Benson remembers that after seven weeks in training camp, much of it spent fighting the flu, he sailed
from Newport News on August 20, 1918 aboard a trans-
port ship. "I think they called it the *Prince Matoka* or
something like that. It had been captured from the
Germans. It took two days just to get the troops aboard.
There seemed like ten thousand of them. The ship was
part of a big convoy. We were near the destroyers that
were around the outside, and one of them sank a German submarine. We landed at Brest on September
third."

Benson missed front-line action by the margin of two
weeks' hospitalization for influenza. Assigned to Company B, 326th Infantry, Eighty-Second Division, he
was moved in late October or early November, 1918 to
an area near Armand about fifty miles from Paris. "We
were just behind the front line. An American airplane
flew over one day and circled around above us. Not
long after that, gas bombs landed in the camp. I got
quite a bit of it but was all right. We found out later
that the airplane was one the Germans had captured.
They flew over us to find out where we were and then
sent in the gas bombs."

Although the armistice came about a week later, Benson was in France until the following May. Embarking for home on May 16, 1919 and landing in Hoboken two weeks later, he had to clear through Camp Marret and Camp Mead. "We got held up an extra day when the trains didn't connect. It seemed the longest day of my life."

Benson's recollection is that "all of those who went from here came back except for Arthur Nelson and Herman Racey. Both of them died in training camp. Arthur was in a truck accident. The flu took Herman. It was the worst enemy most of us had to fight."

Another Yellow Spring war story is about the community's becoming, as it never had before, part of an all-out national endeavor. The public speaking at the Walnut Grove school house on June 27, 1918 was one of a series arranged by the Capon District Precinct Two committee; Vause Whitaker was chairman, Angus R. Spaid assistant chairman, Caudy Davis secretary. Precinct Three had its own committee, headed by George W. Farmer, John Simmons, and E. S. Fletcher; its meetings were held at Mt. Airy. In the June 1918 War Savings Campaign drive, $6,840 was raised in Precinct Two, and $3,230 in Precinct Three. The slogan for the drive was featured in the *Hampshire Review*: "Would You Rather Lend Your Money to Uncle Sam or Pay Tribute to the Kaiser of Germany?"

Marie Brill recalls the gatherings of women, several times a week, to knit sweaters and socks. "We did as many as we could get yarn for but we always wondered how many of them would fit anybody." A report in the January 23, 1918 *Review* from Mrs. Marvin Williams, Secretary of the County Red Cross, confirms the quality control problem. "Some knitters have failed to follow directions and the result is that three pairs of socks had to be raveled out and reknit . . . The things we are most particular about are the heels and toes. The former must not have a ridge under the foot and the toes should not be bound off in a hard ridge. Knots must never be made in wool. . . . A hard ridge or knot will cause blisters and often lead to blood poisoning so we must take every precaution not to chafe the men's feet."

Local women were equally active in the Liberty Loan campaign—a First, Second, then Third, finally a Fourth Drive. Mrs. Turner Monroe was chairman of the Capon District campaign. Her October 1918 statement to the *Review* suggests that the men's vote two years earlier on the Woman's Suffrage Amendment (the count in Romney had been 89 for the amendment, 307 against) had not gone down easily. Referring to the work of the local Liberty Loan committee, she observed bluntly that "when women can fill these kinds of places efficiently it is time for mere men to look to their laurels."

Rationing during World War I was mainly a voluntary local community undertaking. Everybody cut back on the use of goods that were in short supply or were especially needed for shipment to Europe. German submarines prowling off the Florida coast and in the Caribbean meant that sugar stopped coming in from Cuba. Wheat and meat, especially pork, were being sent in huge quantities to England, France, Belgium, Holland.

The February 6, 1918 *Hampshire Review* printed "food rules for West Virginia . . . Fight the Kaiser in the Kitchen. Reduce the Eat in Wheat and Meat." Even the hens were drafted; the Hampshire County Red Cross asked that all eggs laid on Easter Sunday be sent to Romney in order to buy yarn. Governor Cornwell issued a call for "meatless Tuesdays, wheatless Wednesdays, and wasteless everydays," following this up with the proposal to "observe Saturdays as 'Porkless Day' in West Virginia."

For the first time World War I brought to the valley a sense of identity with a national purpose. Independence had only personal meaning here in 1776, and the bloodiness of the 1860s was divisive. Now, almost two centuries after its settlement, Yellow Spring became consciously part of a nation.

About fifteen years before the war, in 1902 or possibly a year earlier, George Davis and his oldest son Carson drove to Waynesburg, Pennsylvania, where the Frick tractor was made, and brought back with them a mobile steam engine. It was the first such vehicle in the valley. Talking about this eighty years later, Carson's son Forrest wonders what it cost. "It must have been the most money the family ever had. But that tractor made one right smart of difference around here."

Stationary steam engines had been used in the valley for a long time. Costing little, they required only a boiler and a simple engine that powered a belt connecting to various machines—a rotary saw or the bark-grinding and roller equipment in the tannery. Steam-powered threshing machines had come in around 1875. But using them meant pulling a boiler and engine and water cart by horse from one field to another, setting up the boiler, building a fire under it and waiting for the steam to come up. Most of the fields were so small that it was barely worth the trouble.

George Davis's Frick tractor, its own wheels powered by the steam generated from the firebed and boiler it carried, changed all of this. A field of grain that used to take a day or more to harvest could now be handled in two or three hours. George and Carson spent several months each year working their Frick on farms up and down the valley.

One of the warmer Davis family stories comes from the time George and both of the older boys were helping with the threshing on a farm at Wardensville belonging to one of the community's leading citizens. When it got dark before the job was done, so that the work couldn't be finished until the next morning, the farmer offered George a bedroom for the night. "The boys," he said, "can bed down in the hayloft." George stood up and started for the door. "If my sons aren't good enough to sleep in your house, sir, we aren't good enough to thresh your wheat." The logic proved compelling.

When Forrest talked, though, of the "right smart of difference" his grandfather's Frick made, he was thinking in broader terms than threshing grain. With a few relatively minor exceptions, this was technology's first entrance on a stage where, for a century and a half, men had relied on their own strength and that of horses to do most of what had to be done, and women on human resources alone.

What followed was a silent, intense drama. This stranger to the valley came bearing unquestionably beneficial gifts, especially labor-saving devices for fields and kitchens alike. But the drummer's wares included, too, instruments that threatened the valley's distinguishing ways of life. With its capacity to both unleash and tyrannize human meaning and purpose, and with no morals of its own, technology challenged people to stay in charge.

By and large this challenge was met, particularly for

one reason. Because there was too little money in the valley to pay for science's marvels when they first came out, technology's advance was kept to an unaccustomed slow pace. The change it brought was gradual enough that it remained manageable.

When a railroad came close to Yellow Spring, it went bankrupt. Work on the Winchester & Western was started in 1916. Coming west from Winchester to Gore along the route of the old Northwest Turnpike (now U.S. Route 50), the right of way turned off beside Willa Cather's home place to follow Back Creek to Shiloh. Cutting over to the Capon, the tracks passed Yellow Spring across the river from the mill, going on then to Wardensville.

Construction on the railroad, seriously underfinanced, moved slowly. Benson LaFollette, who worked on it both before and after the World War, remembers that the pay, regardless of type of job, was $1.50 for a ten-hour day, six days a week. As stable boss, Benson picked up the perk of working seven days instead of six, but the daily rate was the same.

On June 14, 1919 dignitaries from both Richmond and Charleston came out to drive ceremonial spikes (while a band played chorus after chorus of "Blessed Be the Tie that Binds") into the tie under the rails where the W&W crossed the state line. Two years later, construction was completed up to Wardensville. Stations at both Shiloh and Capon Lake served the Yellow Spring area. With Winchester now only two hours away, freight charges low, and a passenger fare of only seventy cents on the two-car rail bus, two centuries of isolation seemed over.

Yellow Spring's imperviousness to progress proved equal to the test. Although the railroad was sometimes

used for shipping out grain from the mill and for bringing in staples for the general store, it proved to be
mostly a logging operation. The quality of passenger
service was reflected in the common translation of
W&W into "Wait or Walk," and the decision was often
close. Declared insolvent in 1926, the railroad, which
became the Winchester and Wardensville, was later
renamed the Winchester and Western under new man-
agement and then was finally closed down, as far as
service west of Gore was concerned, in 1934.

Sometimes it seemed that whatever higher forces
presided over Yellow Spring's destiny were conspiring
deliberately against progress. A bridge was built across
the river in 1924 at Davis Ford. It was constructed of
concrete, not only the piers and roadbed but also the
solid walls along the sides. The large cement slabs
lying beside the ford today are monuments to the capacity of the Capon, so peaceful usually, to become, as
it did in the spring flood of 1936, a sullen, swollen
torrent that makes battering rams of trees riding its
surface. The iron nameplate from the bridge—"Newton
Bridge Company"—which now covers Forrest Davis's
well is a marker to Yellow Spring's resilience to progress. After the bridge collapsed, getting east to Winchester depended again on the river being low enough
to ford.

Automobiles came to Yellow Spring in low, slow
gear. This was partly because the roads here were so
bad. Although the wagon track to Capon Bridge had
been moved in about 1866 from along the base of the
mountains to the level ground beside the river, floods
repeatedly washed it out, and there was a forbiddingly
sharp grade at what is now called, because of the eventual excavation, Dug Hill. Until the new gravel road

(now paved Route 259) was laid and the new bridge was built in the 1930s, Yellow Spring was hard to get to. Or out of.

The principal retarding factor was the automobiles' cost. Raising and keeping horses involved no capital outlay, and steam could be generated by a little wood-splitting. But a car was expensive. So was gasoline. A 1915 advertisement by dealer I.H. Giffin at Capon Bridge listed Model T touring cars at $525 FOB Detroit, sedans at $775, and one-ton trucks at $550. It was front-page news in the *Hampshire Review* for May 26th when Giffin sold "Ford touring cars to Mrs. Mina Cline, Mr. Whitaker and others near Yellow Springs." Since gasoline tractors were too costly for Yellow Spring pocketbooks, the local standard was, up into the 1950s, "a Ford and Frick," the Frick continuing to be the common steam-powered tractor.

If the advanced uses of gasoline power developed slowly in the valley, electricity's marvels were delayed even longer. With one exception. The power required for a local telephone system was available in the dry-cell battery that was part of each instrument, and no central office was needed. As early as the 1880s, the residents of Yellow Spring, Concord, Lehew, Intermont, and Capon Springs strung lines between their homes. Calling a neighbor meant cranking the handle on your own phone to ring the desired number, perhaps "two shorts and a long." The bell rang on every phone in the system. Although only the two-and-one terminal was supposed to answer, clicks on the line reported others tuning in, sometimes so many that the power dimmed until nobody could hear anything.

The system worked well enough except in a storm. The wires were lightning attractors and sparks would spit out of the instrument on the wall. Carson Davis's son Frank recalls his mother gathering her brood together when a thunderstorm came up and huddling them in a corner of the house farthest away from the telephone and the cookstove. "Sparks would come flying out of the phone and make a sizzling beeline for the big iron stove. Mom was scared to death that the house would burn down."

The first "central" system, connecting Yellow Spring with Capon bridge, was installed in 1934 or 1935. Russell Riley got the contract for hauling telephone poles from the road along the river back through the fields and woods to the base of the mountains, where the new line was to be strung. Paid at the rate of ten cents a pole, Russell used a mule, which wasn't common in the valley, and at some points took two hours to move one pole. But there was no hurry. For fifty years the old hand-crank telephone system had met the most strongly felt local need, which was for sociability.

As far as its more significant uses were concerned, "the electric" (a noun in valley usage) reached Yellow Spring from Wardensville in 1935, a century and a half after Benjamin Franklin brought a spark down a wire from the kite he flew into a stormy sky. The original patents had expired on the first Maytags and Frigidaires before these miracles came to the Davises and their neighbors.

Carson Davis, George and Hannah's oldest son, was in his late twenties when he went with his father to Waynesburg and brought back the Frick mobile steam engine that opened technology's revolution in the valley. From the time Carson could lift a hammer he had been George's apprentice in the blacksmithing and

metalworking business. He was fully as good a craftsman and, in his younger brother Caudy's words, "the
most responsible man that ever lived. He took care of
all of us."

Carson's son Forrest tells the Andy Funk story.
George Davis was called on every six months or so to
make repairs on a boiler that Andy, a sawmill operator
who lived back over the mountain, was trying to keep
going beyond normal retirement age. Unable to re-
spond to one of Funk's calls, George sent twelve-year-
old Carson instead. Wanting to do the job right, the
boy made and put in large six-inch staybolts that held
the two walls of the boiler together, reboring holes in
the walls and putting in new patches to prevent leaks.
Carson returned home several days later to report
proudly to his father. "You won't have to worry about
Andy Funk again for a long time." George asked him
what had happened and then, according to the story,
rebuked Carson: "You shouldn't have done all that.
How do you think we're going to keep making a living
here?"

The father and son team did well. Keeping the fire
in the forge down by the river going much of the time,
the two craftsmen moved on from repairing neighbors'
wagons and buggies to turning out models of their own.
They took on Will Lupton to help them, and then, despite his reputation for chronic slow motion, Perry
Peacemaker. "Do you want," Perry asked George one
day, "a flat bevel or a sharp bevel on this chisel?" "From
you, Perry," George answered, "what I want is a fast
bevel." The business prospered.

Remaining unmarried until after his mother's death
in October of 1914, Carson took as his bride two months
later Gladys Franks, daughter of William H. and

Rachel (Farmer) Franks, who lived two miles away, up on the Ridge near Lehew. Carson's sister Cora had married Gladys's brother Hunter and the couple was living in the old Franks place.

Carson and Gladys were not only keepers but builders of the tradition that Samuel and Maria and then George and Hannah had established. Gladys knew when she moved into her new home that her first job was to work out a satisfactory relationship with a father-in-law who had become at this point "considerable cranky," by one report, and, by another, "downright ornery"; George Davis was almost seventy and his joints had stiffened with painful arthritis. Gladys's children remember their mother as having gotten that situation so well in hand that "Mom could handle Grandpa better than Papa could."

Despite their late start, Carson and Gladys raised six children, five to maturity. Thelma Lee was born in 1915, Dorothy Marie in 1918, Charlotte Bell in 1920 (she died at age nine), George Forrest in 1922, Opal Corrine in 1925, Carson Franklin in 1927. Gladys was never strong, and whenever a new Davis showed up Annie Brooks would come over from Parks Hollow to help out. Annie was the daughter of a niece of Hannah's, and George had asked her to come and help first when Hannah was sick. She became a member of the family, Gladys's right hand and friend, and almost a second mother to the children.

First daughter Thelma remembers most clearly the Davis family gatherings at Gladys and Carson's home.

There were several occasions during the years when the family would get together. One time was grape butter making in the fall. Caudy and his wife Ada and their children would come and spend the day. Ada was a delightful person to have around. She was so kind to the children, always in a good mood and making jokes at any problem that came up. Gladys and Ada did the cooking and took care of the small children while the others made the butter. It was a pleasant day and everyone took their share of butter when they left for home.

Gladys would always try to have everybody home for George's birthday. George looked forward to those birthdays. He had a neighbor count the days till his birthday.

Christmas was Annie Brooks's favorite day and she always came back for Christmas with us. When Gladys got sick and was no longer able to take care of things, Annie would come and fix a big Christmas feast. She thought of Gladys and Carson's children as her own.

Carson Davis became a pillar of both family and community. If a brother or sister or son or daughter or neighbor needed help or counsel, they came to him. He kept the family business together. Almost every listing of a community committee includes his name, not as chairman but always present. A cherished family story is of Carson's sitting beside Gladys for a very long time one evening feeding her the small spoonfuls of food that were all she could take, speaking softly, never pressing but going on until what the doctor had said she had to have was finished. Their sons and daughters speak of Gladys and Carson with an almost reverent respect and affection. She died in 1955; he in 1970, at eighty-five. Their graves are at Hebron.

In 1955, their oldest son, Forrest, married Willetta Brill and they moved in to fill the vacuum that Gladys's death had left. Fifth-generation stewards of the Davis and Brill family traditions, Willetta and Forrest are part of most of what happens in Yellow Spring. They and their five children have given two intruders from Washington such neighborly friendship that saying anything more about them would embarrass all of us.

Looking beyond the story of this one family to the broader developments in the valley during the first half of the twentieth century suggests again a theme that has become familiar. This was a period of unprecedented change. Yet this change came at an unaccustomed slow pace. Like most adages, the aphorism about things staying the same only as they change is a half truth. It makes larger sense that the more slowly things change the more nearly they stay the same. Technology came to the valley gradually enough that human values didn't get lost in the rush.

Yet I admit to wondering, perhaps whimsically, whether something beyond this is involved. I have mentioned several times, never fully understanding it, the bond in the valley between people and the land and the river. Could it be that a respect for nature's blessings strengthens a sense of human values against the fallout of technological explosion?

Our neighbor Robin Sirbaugh Davis picked up at auction recently the record of proceedings before local justices of the peace (including both Sirbaughs and Davises) from 1909 to 1950. Going through it affords an interesting reflection of the valley's sense of values and of the attachment between people and nature.

About a third of the recorded items involve men's untoward proceedings against each other. Stot Kerns was charged ten dollars for "Assault and Battery" and Edward Richmond five dollars for "Disturbing the Literary Society".

The substantial majority of the proceedings resulted,

however, from men's offenses against nature. The consequent punishments were significantly larger. U.S. Anderson was fined ten dollars for "Allowing sawdust to enter Capon Spring Run," George W. Bowley twenty dollars when Game Protector B.S. Whitmore found him with "four bass under 8 inches in length," and J.A. LaFollette thirty dollars when he "killed two wild turkeys on the 1 day of November, 1932."

Drawing on rebellious memory, I think it was Aldo Leopold who drew the difference between regarding "land as a commodity belonging to us" and "land as part of the community to which we belong." The idea of ownership is intense here among people whose families have lived for generations in the valley. But the concept goes beyond ownership. It is more like a sense of citizenship, including a loyalty to the land and to the river—and a healthy suspicion of Technology and Progress as aliens or at best questionable characters.

Mister Caudy

Named for a legendary Indian fighter and for a
father born to the soil, Caudy George Davis decided
early to follow his own course. Almost a century later,
his son Charles said in affectionate epitaph, "Dad was
the most independent cuss that ever lived."

In conversations that became over the years a weekend ritual, Jane and I sometimes tried to get at what
had led George and Hannah Davis's third son, born on
April 30, 1886, to break away in so many respects from
the traditional family pattern—and yet to remain at
the same time a vital part of both that family and this
community. Mister Caudy didn't make it easy. Whenever the talk got close to his own childhood he closed
the door. Only once, when Jane asked him about his
"oldest recollection," did he open a small window.

Hesitating so long that we thought he wasn't going
to answer, he finally replied with surprising directness.
"Yes, I remember my mother making me my first pair
of pants. She cut them down from a pair of Carson's or

Tom's. And I remember that when she put them on me I ran off and hid behind the rosebush." Then he stopped.

"Because you wanted your own new ones," Jane prompted.

"No. Because I wanted to wear my baby clothes. And I did, even when they laughed at me."

"Did your mother laugh at you?"

"No. It was the others. But I didn't care." Then he turned the conversation to something else.

On the way home, Jane and I decided that what the old master had done, with characteristic subtlety, was put into a simple anecdote the critical elements of a much broader story that he wasn't going to go into. Jane mused about whether it was at the prompting of an errant gene or because of some happenstance of infancy that a very small rebel decided never to wear anybody else's trousers. He never did.

Not long after the sartorial crisis an even more significant form of waywardness showed up. By the time he was five or six, the youngest Davis had started reading and writing and begging to go to school. No previous sign of any comparable malady had appeared in generations of Davis, Spaid, Switzer, or Kline boys.

Looking back later on "never missing a day of school in eight years," the assiduous scholar put equal importance on "not being interested just in book learning." He and arithmetic had fallen in love on first meeting. One of his teachers, Caudy Nixon from Capon Bridge, located a compass and a surveyor's chain that didn't cost much. Older brother Carson came up with the necessary funds, as he did so often in other connections. Learning about metes and bounds "from books, by kerosene lamp, and pine knots in the fire," Caudy laid out imaginary plats on the mountainside back of the house and in the fields and woods across the river. By the time he was twelve, he was surveying for his neighbors.

Despite the increasing restlessness he felt, young Caudy stayed in filial harness until he was eighteen, working long days with his father and brothers in the fields and tannery and down at the forge. Low man on what he considered not much of a totem pole, he didn't like it. By this time he realized that the two houses and the property would eventually go to his brothers, Carson and Tom. As third son he would have to find something else.

A short stint as a mail handler on the Baltimore and Ohio Railroad helped make two things clear. "I wanted," he summed it up many years later, "to use my head as well as my hands. But I realized that I didn't want to leave the valley."

In the summer of 1904, looking for some way to reconcile his objectives, Caudy enrolled in a three-month teaching preparatory course offered by a Professor Elosser at Bean's Settlement near North River fifteen miles over the mountain. Tuition was eight dollars a month, and room and board with one of the Bean families about that much more. Going to Romney at the end of the summer to take the teacher examination ("All you had to be able to do was add two and two and write your name"), Caudy signed on for that winter at the Walnut Grove School, in his own side yard. After a second summer with Professor Elosser, he taught at Walnut Grove one more winter, spent three years at the Sudan School on North River, and then another at Red Bud School, over on Back Creek.

Each year the young schoolmaster had "about eighteen students, but it always depended on the weather.

Most of them were between the ages of six and twelve, a few older, one or two about sixteen or seventeen."

The principal problems were "discipline and motivation. I could handle the first all right. They knew who was in charge."

"Did you ever use a ruler?"

"Only to measure with," he laughed. "I did spank two of the older ones once. They were trying to cut up." Although he didn't supply the details, this may have been the time when, as local tradition relates, Clarence Pennington and Ross Cline came to school one morning with cheeks contoured by small quids of chewing tobacco. As teacher Davis started toward Ross, the miscreant turned around and deposited his wad in an envelope he had provided for such an emergency. Co-conspirator Clarence, less foresighted, swallowed the evidence—with consequences that tradition doesn't touch on.

"Motivation was harder. Truancy wasn't even thought of; they just came or they didn't, depending on the weather and what had to be done at home. They took to simple arithmetic, for they could see the use for it, and some geography and history. But spelling didn't seem important to them, and nobody had any use for grammar. They wanted to be able to read and maybe write what they would have to. Anything beyond that didn't take. It was frustrating, and I gave it up. This was really, though, because of the money."

There was clearly more to it than low pay. Children's uncanny knack for learning what they think they are going to be able to use meant that Caudy Davis and his colleagues faced an almost impossible task. They could scratch the ground and plant seeds—for less pay than they would have received for the commonest labor. Armetha Haines Carrier, whose own schooling started in 1907 and who spent thirty-six years teaching throughout the area, puts the problem succinctly: "We did what we could. But teaching boys and girls to be book-smarter than their dads and moms was pretty hard when you had to do it alone."

In 1906, when he was twenty and still teaching school during the winter months, young Caudy started reaching out in another direction. There was an open term for justice of the peace, or district magistrate as it was more commonly known, for the eastern district of Hampshire County, which included Yellow Spring. "The two candidates on the ballot were John Schaffnaker and one of the Orndorffs from Capon Spring. I wasn't on the ballot but said I would run. They went after each other and both got chewed up. I believe I got more votes than the two of them put together, although I am not sure about this."

The magistrates were assigned cases by the County Court, usually three or four a month. Most of Magistrate Davis's hearings were held in the Walnut Grove schoolhouse.

"A lot of my cases came from the Bloomery district. The people there were rougher. One squabble was about a piece of personal property, between an old lady and a young woman about twenty-five. One was about as bad as the other, but the younger woman was right. The old lady had gone after her with a club. I gave the property to the young woman and fined the old lady. Then I 'sentenced' the girl to going to Sunday School every Sunday for I don't remember now how long. It worked. People from the neighborhood told me later she became a fine, upright woman."

The young justice's most serious problem involved

a dispute between his uncle, Jefferson Davis, and John Schaffnaker, whom Caudy had defeated for the magistrate's office. Although the case involved a commonplace complaint—that Jeff's chickens had developed a habit of taking their meals in neighbor John's oatfield—the complications were considerable, including not only the justice's relationships with both men but the additional fact that the plaintiff and the defendant had married sisters, daughters of Alfred Anderson. Jeff and his wife Angie had moved in with her father.

When the case was brought to him, Justice Davis advised the litigants that under the circumstances he couldn't decide it himself. He suggested that each disputant select an arbitrator and that those two pick a third. "They agreed to this. Jeff picked Smith Brill, John Schaffnaker chose one of the Luptons, and together they named Will Johnson, the miller.

"A lot of interest had developed, and there was a whale of a crowd, like someone was getting married. I had a time keeping it all under control. At one point, Uncle Jeff said he wanted to ask Alfred Anderson, his father-in-law and also John Schaffnaker's, a question. I let him do it, which was a mistake. Uncle Jeff's question was 'Why do you think John is giving me such a hard time?' And Alfred answered, 'I guess, Jeff, it's because you've been getting better corn than he has.'

"Alfred was clearly on Jeff's side, and he kept trying to butt in. He was sitting right beside me and I had to keep punching him in the ribs. Finally I said, 'Mr. Anderson, unless you keep quiet I will have to fine you for contempt of this court.' That shut him up.

"Then Uncle Jeff asked that the three arbitrators visit the property, which they did. When they came back, Smith Brill had written out a decision. There was a brief statement of facts. Then he read 'We therefore contend and do hereby report that the damage objected to is only what one farmer might rightly expect from another.' It was signed by all three."

Although he enjoyed being a magistrate, Caudy didn't stand for re-election at the end of his term. A new interest demanded a broader and firmer income than part-time schoolteaching and adjudicating provided.

Caudy had always known the Nicholas and Sarah Spaid family who lived across the river, about a mile back up Crooked Run Road from where the Ell Ridge schoolhouse stood (still does, barely) beside the county road. Nicholas Spaid, like Caudy's mother, traced his line, but by a different route, back to the Hessian mercenary, George Spaht. His wife had been an Anderson, her mother a LaFollette.

The Nicholas Spaid family, which included eleven children, lived plainly, their daily pattern dominated by Sarah's strong Dunkard convictions. Every Sunday, in all except the bitterest weather, the whole family drove fifteen miles over the mountains to the Church of the Brethren at Pleasant Dale, near Augusta. Sons Angus and Daniel became ministers, and three of the girls went to the Brethren's College in Bridgewater, Virginia.

The ninth of the eleven Spaid children, second cousins to George and Hannah Davis's four children, was born on November 28, 1887 and christened Ada Eleanor. Spaid genealogist Albert Thompson Secrest describes Ada as particularly vivacious, which other fuller accounts attest to. She was one of the three sisters who had attended college at Bridgewater, and after finishing her course she stayed on briefly as a teacher.

On June 6, 1912, Caudy George Davis, then twenty-six, and Ada Eleanor Spaid, twenty-five, were married. We asked Mister Caudy one day when his sons Charles and Sam were also there, to tell us about it. Smiling a little, he didn't reply at first. "Where was the ceremony?" someone prompted. The smile broadened and he answered concisely: "Beside the gate at the Good place, up the road here."

"No," we laughed, "not your courting, your marrying."

"Oh, there were witnesses."

"Was there a minister?"

"Oh, yes. I had arranged for him to meet us there."

"What time of day? Or night?"

"High noon."

Sam went upstairs and brought down the framed marriage certificate. The presiding cleric was Reverend S. G. Thomas, Pastor of M. E. Church South; the witnesses were Letisha Thomas and Lucille Anderson. Letisha was probably the pastor's wife, and Lucille represented Ada's mother's family. Asked whether there were any other Davises present, Mister Caudy smiled again.

"No, indeed." We didn't press him. He wouldn't have said anything more if we had.

The Good farm is on the line between Hampshire and Hardy counties. Caudy and Ada had gotten their marriage license in Romney, the Hampshire county seat, but because Pastor Thomas, who was from Hardy County, was concerned about whether his commission carried across the county line, he stood on it as he accepted the young couple's vows.

After the ceremony, Ada and Caudy got in a buggy and drove to Winchester; "down across the river at

Davis Ford, past the schoolhouse, then up the ridge and east to Lockharts hill, which was twice as steep as now because the road dipped down into the ravine on the left, then came back up." Taking the train at Winchester for Harpers Ferry and then into Washington, they spent their honeymoon at the home of Ada's two sisters.

Mr. Caudy's reported highlights of the trip aren't romantic. "We looked at all those big government buildings, and we went by a bookstore that had piles of books on tables out on the sidewalk. They were used books, but not very much. I got a trigonometry book and another on geometry for sixty cents." Sylvia, Caudy's daughter, recalls that her mother most enjoyed their visit to Mt. Vernon.

Caudy and Ada returned from their honeymoon to an uncertain future in the valley. His teaching brought about $150 a year, and as magistrate he received only occasional case fees. When their first child, Charles Galen, was born, on August 7, 1913, while Ada and Caudy were staying with her parents over on Crooked Run Road, the young couple knew they needed more money.

Caudy found his opportunity, again with brother Carson's help, when the mill at Yellow Spring came up for sale in the winter of 1913-1914. Once a flourishing business, the mill had run into problems, including a fire ("the insurance policy got pretty hot") and several changes of ownership. The machinery was barely working. The Davis brothers bought the mill from Ashbury Frank and D. W. Griffin for $4,000. One of the sellers owed Carson $200, and when Caudy scraped together his share they had their down payment. The house close to the mill came with the deal, and Caudy and Ada and their infant son moved in there shortly after the purchase.

If his earlier life suggested an aversion to hard labor, the new mill operator's work habits dispelled the illusion. Working the sixteen-hour-a-day schedule he would keep for the next fifty years, all of his time went into getting the mill back in shape. The business had to be rebuilt from scratch and the miller's take was small. Limiting the operation at first to grinding up for feed whatever grain was brought in, he moved into milling flour, meal, and what one advertisement called "kindred milling products." A bushel of wheat yielded the grower forty pounds of flour, six or seven of bran (which went to the cattle and horses), and three or four of "midlins" (for the pigs). The remaining ten pounds of grain were the miller's toll.

How far the "kindred milling products" phrase reached was a family joke. A stillhouse back of the mill permitted transforming grain into its more exhilarating forms. One version of the story is that the product was offered as a come-on to customers. Mister Caudy's protests that "we never sold the stuff" leave some uncertainty about whether this was a matter of principle or because there was too much local do-it-yourself competition. When the cooker on the still got too hot one day and blew up, it wasn't replaced.

Caudy eventually bought up Carson's interest in the mill, paying him off over an extended period of years. Installing a new thirty-foot overshot iron millwheel permitted not only the more efficient operation of the mill but the generation of enough electricity to lessen Ada's washing and ironing chores. Carson's son Frank recalls with more clarity than Caudy's son Sam the cousins' experiment one night when the miller was away. They opened up the small gate that controlled the flow of water over the wheel, causing the speeded-up generator to blow every bulb in the mill and house and in the store across the road, permitting the misdemeanants' escape under cover of darkness.

In 1918, Caudy rented the general store from Asa Cline, bought up the inventory, and ran both the store and the mill for the next two years. One of the fringe benefits was serving as postmaster. The resourceful merchant was not above disposing of some slow-moving fabric, which had been priced at six cents a yard, by marking it "Special Sale. Full bolt only 9¢/yard," and calling the bargain to Mrs. Schaffnaker's personal attention. But a private note in his ledger reflects Caudy's increasing exasperation with some of his customers' slight regard for paying their bills, and in 1920 he sold the store to Winfred and Ross Cline.

I wish I could tell in equal detail the story of Ada Spaid Davis. Mister Caudy kept this room, too, tightly locked, marked "Private." But their children's stories make it clear that Ada did her job as well as Caudy did his.

There were four boys and two girls. Charles (born in 1913) was followed by Helen Angeline (1917), Cornwell Woodrow (1919), Sylvia Katherine (1923), Sterling George (1925), and Samuel Price (1930).

Benson LaFollette describes Ada as "a beautiful woman, short, just a little heavyset, warm, always kind of glowing." She did most of the children's rearing. Charles recalled that his father "wouldn't stop working for dinner, and Mom would have to call him two or three times to come in for supper. He was at the mill or store before we left for school in the morning and when we came home in the evening."

Sam remembers his mother as "the foundation on which we were raised. She was strict in some cases, but always understanding and sympathetic. She carried a heavy load, but she never seemed to show, on the outside, any unhappiness or sadness."

The family was extended in the mid-1920s to include Ada's sisters, Bertha and Elvie. They took over the house that had come with the mill, and Caudy and Ada and their children moved into a new home (the mill office today) built next door. Although Sam immortalizes his aunts as "two saints," a redeeming earthly character was reflected in their painting the walls of the living room with large, varicolored polka dots; "to take our minds," Elvie explained, "off the rheumatiz." The broader community recollection is of the "three Spaid girls" as sharing heavenly attributes including a talent for cookery and an uncommon warmth and good humor.

The young Davises' schooling, like their father's, was at Walnut Grove, which meant a mile-and-a-quarter walk each way. They would be joined by John and Madge Kline, Madison and Abbie Kline's children, and Abbie always had cookies and milk or cocoa ready for them on the way home in the afternoon. By this time, school had become more serious business, being held for seven months—until it was cut back again to five when the Depression came along in 1930.

A high school was built at Capon Bridge in 1924. Getting to it from Yellow Spring meant two long rides each school day in Dave Franks's bus—an old Model T paneled Ford truck, retired from more demanding service, with bench seats along the sides. Dave, living on the other side of the river, met his passengers each morning at Davis Ford, except when high water washed out the day's education.

Arriving home from school meant getting to work on chores around the house, at the mill, or on a nearby piece of property that Caudy was farming. As a boy, he had felt resentment that for his father "the only question was labor," but in his own manhood and parenting he treated losing a minute as a misdemeanor. He drove himself hard, with long days at the mill leading to more hours after dark at his standup desk. The subjects of his fatherly discipline remember it as "fair and even but very, very firm."

Caudy Davis might well have sat down at his desk the evening of April 30, 1926 to take inventory. It was his fortieth birthday. He would have listed, at least in his mind, both financial and personal debits and credits.

The credits were clear. Business at the mill, hub of Yellow Spring's modest economy, had so improved that Caudy had recently become a charter stockholder in the new Western Frederick Bank at Gore. Ada and the children were well. The house had gotten too small, but Caudy and Ada had plans to build a new home across the road. Assets clearly exceeded liabilities.

There was one debit item. The successful-at-forty teacher, magistrate, storekeeper, and mill owner realized that he wasn't satisfied. Having established his personal pattern of aspirations and measuring success by his own standards, he hadn't yet found what he was looking for. So he reset his sights.

Ten years earlier, Caudy had dabbled in local Democratic politics, making informal speeches and raising a few dollars for Herman Guy Kump, who had grown up over on Loman's Branch and was running for the State Assembly. With Woodrow Wilson heading up the national ticket, 1916 was a good enough year that previously Republican West Virginia elected as governor Democrat John J. Cornwell, editor of the *Hampshire Review*. Kump won easily. Of the 131 votes cast at the Walnut Grove and Mt. Airy polling places, 106 were for the Democratic ticket. In a referendum on women's suffrage, the men voted 105-8 (with eighteen open-minded or timid abstentions) that women belonged at home. Caudy Davis only smiled when he was asked sixty-five years later how he voted on the referendum.

In the 1922 election, the miller had put even more time into Burr Saville's candidacy for sheriff of Hampshire County, and when it was successful Saville appointed Caudy deputy sheriff for the Capon and Bloomery districts. His official duties meant making new acquaintances and friends, and shortly before his fortieth birthday, Caudy had announced his candidacy as delegate from Hampshire County to the West Virginia legislature.

During the primary campaigning the political novice's chances seemed slim at first. But the well-known incumbent, O. B. Cullinan from Springfield, didn't take seriously enough the threat of the miller and deputy sheriff from the little community of Yellow Spring, over in a corner of the county. Winning the primary, Caudy Davis breezed through the general election and went to Charleston in January 1927 as Hampshire's new delegate. The next four years (he was virtually unopposed for a second term starting in 1929) brought him very close to his dreams.

During the biennial sessions, scheduled for sixty days but usually extended, either Cecil or Dave Long, Caudy's neighbors and friends, took over the mill. The delegate pay was modest, $500 a year salary plus ten cents a mile for travel back and forth to the sessions in Charleston. While some of his colleagues, he told me one day, "came there without the price of a hotel room and drove away in Cadillacs," the delegate from Hampshire County, "wasn't ever offered a penny. They knew it wouldn't be taken."

A freshman delegate from Hampshire County, outside of West Virginia's coal country, had a hard time establishing an influence base. One of thirty-one Democratic delegates in a House that included sixty-three Republicans, his committee assignments were ordinary: Federal Relations, Redistricting, and Humane Institutions and Public Buildings. Yet he managed to author, introduce, and carry through to passage, in the 1929 session, the Worthless Check Law—"House Bill No. 80—By Mr. Davis."

Although passing bad checks had never been officially condoned in West Virginia, the loopholes built into the old law and the lightness of the penalties that were imposed made kiting a common form of scalawaggery—until House Bill No. 80 became law on June 2, 1929.

> Any person who, with intent to defraud, shall make, draw, issue, utter or deliver any check . . . upon any bank . . . and thereby obtain . . . any credit, credit on account, money, goods or other property or thing of value knowing at the time . . . that the maker or drawer thereof has not sufficient funds in, or credit with such bank . . . shall be guilty of a misdemeanor . . . [if the check is for less than $20] . . . or a felony [if $20 or over].

Passing worthless checks was condemned as "against the peace and dignity of the state," subject to penalties of $100 to $1,000 and from five days in jail to five years in the penitentiary. If the 1929 enactment didn't put an end to such offenses against West Virginia's peace and dignity, the practice proved a good deal less popular than it had been before the delegate from Hampshire County spelled out its hazards.

Another piece of delegate Davis's legislating would let him point later out the window of his home, beside State Route 259, and say "I guess you could call me the daddy of that road." Which is right. It ought to be named for him.

The story started in the late 1920s when the citizens of Wardensville insisted that as residents of the largest town in the Capon Valley they were entitled to a road to Winchester suitable for automobile travel. The original proposal had been to route a new highway through Strasburg, Virginia (following the course chosen later for U.S. 55).

The delegate from Hampshire County came up with a different idea. An alternative to the Strasburg route was to go from Wardensville to Winchester by way of Yellow Spring. Learning of a hearing set by the Virginia Department of Highways to consider the matter, delegate Davis drove over to the meeting at Harrisonburg to make "probably my most effective speech except maybe the one on the bad check law. I pointed out that the West Virginia State Farm [on the road from Wardensville to Yellow Spring] deserved service. Then I emphasized what really counted with the Virginia Highway Department. The Wardensville-to-Strasburg route would be on the east side of North Mountain, which would mean that Virginia would have to pay for most of the road building, but the Yellow Spring route would put most of the cost on West Virginia."

Carrying the day at Harrisonburg, the young assemblyman ran into an unexpected problem at home. He had planned that the new road follow the river all the way from Wardensville through Yellow Spring to Capon Bridge, to join up there with the Romney-to-Winchester road (now U.S. Route 50). But he found that the farmers below Yellow Spring took a dim view of a new "improved road" coming their way. The dirt road along the river met their needs, and improving it would mean giving up more of their fields. All for Progress, they didn't want it routed through their own pastures.

Taking counsel with his brother Carson, who at one point went back with Caudy to Charleston, the delegate came up with an innovative and preferable alternative. The shortest route to Winchester would be to bridge the river near the mill at Yellow Spring, go up on the Ridge, and then join at Lehew with the right-of-way that was already in use. Doing the necessary lobbying with Carson's help, delegate Davis got his proposed route approved. Work began quickly and by 1933 there was a new bridge at Yellow Spring and a good gravel road up and along the Ridge. The wages from building them helped carry this area through the national depression that had hit just as construction was starting.

Standing for reelection in 1930, incumbent delegate Davis was defeated in the primary by Ira V. Cowgill, a veteran Democrat and a judge from Romney. When I asked about this, Mr. Caudy said something about "not being able to afford electioneering," but stopped when he realized that he seemed to be making excuses.

Incomplete reports in the *Hampshire Review* suggest several elements in the 1930 defeat. Caudy Davis's otherwise gracious post-election statement includes an enigmatic passage: "While some last minute reports were untrue . . .." I think the nub of the story is that opponent Cowgill was from Romney, where so many of the voters lived. The Romney precinct came in 297 for Cowgill, 135 for Davis. This difference was close to Cowgill's winning majority in the county as a whole; Davis carried most of the outlying precincts.

A shortage of campaign funds was probably an additional factor. The mill faced serious financial problems. The national depression, triggered by the November 1929 stock market crash, was only beginning to be felt in the valley. But people here still refer to 1930 as "the year of the big drought." In the column next to the one carrying the defeated candidate's concession statement in the *Review* for August 13, 1930 is a story reporting that "the ministers of Romney have planned a union prayer service at the Methodist Church next Wednesday evening at eight o'clock to petition our Heavenly Father to send rain upon the thirsty land."

The rain didn't come until September, which was too late. There was no corn and very little small grain. Mister Caudy told us once how "nobody had any money. Day after day the mill wouldn't do fifty cents worth of business. I didn't owe anything. That was something to be thankful for. But I didn't have any cash reserve and money was so tight I didn't know where to turn."

Although he never suggested it himself, the combination of local drought and national depression probably explains the move, otherwise hard to understand, that Caudy made in 1933. When his friend Herman Kump, who had become governor of the state, offered him a four-year term as deputy state tax commissioner, he took it. The decision couldn't have been easy. His office was to be in the state capital in Charleston but the family was to stay in Yellow Spring. Sam was a toddler and three of the other children were under fifteen. Ada already had her hands terribly full.

This went on for eight years, the new West Virginia governor, Homer A. Holt, renewing Caudy's appointment in 1937. He recalled this service later with satisfaction strongly diluted by regret about being away from home and living in hotels; "four of them . . . all the same . . . one room . . . pretty bare." But his duties meant being in the field quite a bit of the time, and the territory he covered—Grant, Hampshire, Hardy, Mineral, and Pendleton counties—was close to Yellow Spring.

In 1940, a bitter factional fight developed within the state Democratic party between Governor Holt's "State Housers," who were supporting Carl Andrews to succeed Holt, and "the Federals," whose candidate for governor was U.S. Senator M.M. Neely. Holt made a radio speech in April in which he charged that Neely was a puppet of John L. Lewis and the United Mine Workers and an advocate of "totalitarian, tyrannical, and despotic concepts of government." Neely dismissed Holt and Andrews and their supporters as "the Mental Midgets."

Winning handily in the primary, and coasting through the general election when Franklin D. Roosevelt trounced Wendell Willkie, newly ensconced Governor Neely followed the usual procedures. "He made a speech," Mister Caudy recalled, "about letting bygones be bygones. But before very long, we knew we were the ones that were goners." In August of 1941, the new deputy tax commissioner for the five counties was Vernon Whitacre from High View, another former schoolteacher and surveyor, who had supported Neely and who later became a state senator.

Accepting the change as part of political custom, the newspapers in the area carried editorial compliments a tax collector doesn't expect or often get:

In the *Grant County Press*: We've had for about eight years in this district a representative from the tax commissioner's office, one C. G. Davis, of Hampshire County, who would jog us up on our taxes. He had a way of doing it that, in the language of one of our citizens, it was a pleasure to pay them. He played no favorites, but knew his people, spoke their language and was a most efficient official.

In the *Mineral Daily News-Tribune* (Keyser): The political axe has caught up with an old friend of ours. C. G. Davis, deputy state tax collector for this area, was relieved of his duties on August 1. Caudy, whose home is over at Yellow Spring in Hampshire county, is well known in Keyser and Mineral county and he probably knows as many people here as most of the natives. There are about one thousand persons in this county who pay state taxes and Caudy can call eighty percent of them by their first names. He was always obliging in helping fill out income tax and other blanks and we doubt if even his political enemies could find anything wrong with his work.

In the *Hampshire Review*: Caudy G. Davis . . . retires with regrets from the people of the several counties he has served so well. Always he has been one of the outstanding citizens of this county.

Former Governor Kump wrote personally: "I want you to know, Caudy, that I think you rendered excellent service, and I am glad that you were connected with the Administration while I was at the statehouse and also under my successor. I congratulate you upon the service you rendered, and upon attaining the high regard and confidence of the people with whom you came in contact. With best wishes to you and your loved ones. . . ."

The retiring tax collector replied to these extraordinary encomiums in the September 17, 1941 issue of the *Review*:

It has been my happy privilege to contact in my official capacity some three thousand persons yearly who pay some form of taxes to the state, beside many individuals I learned to know in the territory assigned me . . .

No doubt it may be some time before I have the opportunity of seeing many of my friends, but I want all to know that you have been an inspiration to me and I shall always remember the many kindnesses you have so generously accorded me in the execution of my duties.

Sincerely,
Caudy G. Davis

This exchange of compliments came at the end of a period when it had been harder for people to pay their taxes than ever before. You wonder whether there is any comparable recognition of a revenuer's performance, any other footnote in American history that says better what public service in a democracy is supposed to mean.

These developments left, though, a void in the faithful servant's personal affairs, and a hard and critical choice. "It was the only time," Mister Caudy said later, "that I ever felt at loose ends." Coming back to the mill "didn't seem fair. Charles was in charge there now and Cornwell was helping him. And I had done all that before."

He stayed on in Charleston for several months as an

abstractor in the Land Department in the State Auditor's office. "But this was dreary business. It was hard to get home. It did give me time to think about what I wanted to do, and gradually I realized that I had known all along—ever since I was in school and Caudy Nixon, my teacher, found that compass and chain and Carson loaned me the money to buy them."

When Caudy and Ada had built their new home in 1935, across River Road from the mill, the first-floor room fronting on what is now Route 259 had been designed for possible commercial use. Making an ideal office and workroom, it was for the next twenty years the headquarters of "Caudy G. Davis, Surveyor."

Returning with characteristic zest to the occupation that had intrigued him ever since he was a boy, the surveyor quickly picked up more business than he could handle, even in workdays that still started at dawn and continued until after dark. His first-name knowing of three thousand taxpayers in five counties helped. It counted more that surveyor Davis had a reputation for being as careful about each minute within each degree on a compass, and about a six-inch measurement along a 160-pole line, as he had been about a single cent on a dollar that somebody owed the state government.

We sometimes spent an afternoon going through the file drawers of abstracts and related letters and documents that filled a corner of his office. His clients, mostly individuals whose affairs were minor but also corporations with substantial interests at stake, had clearly been afforded equal attention and care. The correspondence shows that the surveyor was relied on as counselor and sometimes arbitrator as well. When I mentioned this recently to Kenneth Seldon, the admired and beloved keeper of the general store for over thirty years and Mister Caudy's closest friend in many respects, it reminded Kenneth of the help he had gotten when he bought the store in 1952. "I didn't really know Mr. Davis then and he wasn't involved in any way. But I was going to be his neighbor and that was enough. He went over every angle of it, asking the questions I should have thought of but hadn't. He was the most careful man I ever knew."

When I chided Mister Caudy a little once about his meticulous worksheets and the cross-checking of calculations on a relatively small matter, he came close to taking offense. "I was being paid to be right. If I was wrong, I was cheating somebody."

A notation on one of his billings, "For services rendered at $2.50/hour," prompted my further impudence that twenty dollars a day seemed terribly low. He corrected my arithmetic. "I hardly ever stopped short of twelve hours. It was usually closer to fifteen, including of course my office time. Fifty or seventy-five dollars for a survey was a lot to people around here, and I didn't think it was fair to charge others more." Charles Davis commented once that his father "could have been a wealthy man. He just never seemed to care much at all about money."

In late October of 1961, Ada Davis, who had never been in a hospital, had to have a tumor removed. There were postoperative complications and she died on November 2nd. When I asked Mister Caudy whether Ada "had a hard time of it," he shook his head slowly—and said nothing. Respecting his feeling about this, it is appropriate to say only that as far as I can tell Ada Spaid Davis was the most beloved woman in the community—because, I think, she never let anything get her down.

At the time of Ada's death, Caudy was seventy-five. Five of his sons and daughters were living, three of them close by. Sterling had been killed in World War II. One of the first young men in the area to be drafted, he became a paratrooper, was sent to Holland, and died in action on October 5, 1944. Mister Caudy kept Sterling's picture and the Silver Heart certificate over his desk. He never talked about it.

Charles had married Francis Jordan, and he and Cornwell, whose wife had been Helen Elizabeth McKee, were running the mill. Helen and her husband Willard Riley had their home up on the Ridge. Sylvia, after marrying Wallace Forrester, had moved to Madison in Boone County. Samuel had married Mabel Eunice Larrick, a teacher in the Frederick County school system; living in Winchester, they came out frequently for weekends.

Mister Caudy's decision to stay on, alone, in the big white house, may have been easier for him than it would be for most men. He had known loneliness as a child. No family member had been at his wedding. The nine years when he was based in Charleston, spending most of his weeknights in a dreary hotel room, reflected an unusual self-sufficiency. A human warmth that three thousand citizens could feel even in a tax collector was masked behind considerable reserve.

Two months after Ada's death, however, the surveyor put away his rod and chain and compass and closed his books. His later explanation that he had to—"my knees gave out"—was unquestionably part of it. My guess, though, is that his feeling tired for the first time in his life came equally from realizing that without Ada what he was doing had lost its meaning.

Yet no thought of giving up, except for what the aching in his knees demanded, entered Caudy Davis's thinking. Having done well every job he had undertaken as a matter of choice, he set out deliberately to perform with distinction life's remaining assignment—which imposes its own terms.

Enlivening Geriatric Bitters

At their regularly scheduled first-Tuesday-of-the-month meeting on May 1, 1984, the day after Caudy Davis's ninety-eighth birthday, the directors of the Western Frederick Bank re-elected him chairman of the board. Missing the meeting, he apologized later to his colleagues that the calendar's quirk, putting May's first Tuesday on the opening day of the month, "tricked me." The fuller truth came out in a more private conversation. "I didn't want my being there to make them think they had to do me a favor."

In his own view of it, retirement was the hardest job the former teacher, miller, legislator, tax collector summa cum laude, meticulous surveyor ever had. Life at less than hard labor, mental and physical alike, seemed to him cruel and unusual punishment. Yet he will probably be remembered longest for the way he graced the business of growing old.

Apprentices ourselves in this demanding and hazardous occupation, Jane and I have compared notes from time to time about the master craftsman's handling of it. Although the central element of his art is clear we disagree a little about how to characterize it. In Jane's view, the ninety-eight-year old president of the bank board who played hooky from the meeting because he didn't want any favors done him was the same "independent cuss" who had objected a century earlier to wearing somebody else's pants. I want to call it not only independence but pride, which puts in a slightly different perspective both his going his own way and also his relentless keeping up to snuff by the standards and ideals he had set, very high, for himself.

If pride has an overtone of vanity, Mister Caudy would necessarily have pled guilty to traces of that vice. Or at least nolo contendere, no contest. Bald almost from youth, he wore a hat whenever the circumstances permitted, often indoors. Sitting in the patriarch's place at a Davis family reunion on an August Sunday when both he and the temperature were well over ninety, he wore the only jacket and necktie in the room. Joshed a little about it, he confessed to "thinking somebody might be taking pictures."

Caudy Davis always drove the biggest automobile in Yellow Spring, usually in contempt of speed limits. His first car, bought before he could afford it, was a Reo. Charles recalled from his early childhood an after-dark dash for home from Wardensville. "Dad was driving too fast for that dirt road, which was along the foot of the mountain then. The Reo had carbide lights and they weren't much count. Bessie Brill's cow was out and Dad ran smack into her. Busted the carbide lamp but didn't hurt the cow. We helped her up and she went off bawling." Later Caudy owned a Buick and finally a large black Cadillac. Intent even in his nineties on pushing the accelerator as hard as he could, to the family's despair and the sheriff's cumulative annoyance, the pilot finally had to be grounded.

A higher form of pride was reflected when we dropped by Mister Caudy's home on cold, rainy mornings that almost committed him to solitary confinement. He sat reading in his chair by the window, clean shaven, neatly sweatered, always wearing a carefully knotted necktie. When Jane brought him a loaf of homemade hobo bread or a jar of rose-geranium jelly he would protest his not having anything for her in return. The amenities were important to him.

If these were superficial things, some others weren't. Listening more clinically than was fair as he talked, we realized that his words, always simple, were chosen carefully and structured into complete sentences that honored grammar's strictest rules. No infinitive was ever fractured, no participle left dangling, no preposition left stranded at the end of a sentence. He didn't misuse "hopefully." No colloquialisms in pronunciation crept in. His occasional restrained but sometimes pungent expletives were tailored rather than custommade. I never saw a misspelled word on even his roughest worksheets or a calculation that stopped short of two decimal points, three if they mattered.

When I asked Mister Caudy too bluntly one day where he got his standards, he took legitimate offense, asking what I meant. I only made things worse by mentioning that he had developed a self-mastery of the English language and of trigonometry from a Walnut Grove base. He probably found the question condescending, which was far from its intention. In any event it was none of my business, and he never gave me an answer.

Jane's independence theory does explain better some pieces that have to be fitted in: the young man's going his own different way; the miller's not coming in for supper until the third call; the tax collector's being willing to pay the price of nine years away from home; his steadfast insistence on continuing to live alone in a house much too big for him. Perhaps pride and independence are at their best an ineffable blend. They were the essence of Caudy Davis's Enlivening Geriatric Bitters.

Another clearly identifiable element in his fourth-quarter game plan was Faith, in both of its meanings, lower and upper case. As one meaning ran out on him, he relied increasingly on the other.

During the early years of our talking together, often about politics, we found common ground in the shared persuasion that "things were getting better." An ardent Democrat, Mister Caudy greatly admired John Kennedy and Lyndon Johnson. Although Hubert Humphrey had lost an election to Richard Nixon, it was easy enough to put this down at the time as a temporary setback. Jay Rockefeller's star was rising in West Virginia and, despite some reservation about "rich men's sons," Mister Caudy viewed the situation in Charleston as promising.

Very conscious of the general economic improvement in Appalachia, especially along the Capon, Mister Caudy was proud that Democratic policy had contributed to this. Traffic had gotten much heavier along the road he properly considered partly his own achievement. Houses in the community that had become eyesores were being repainted or rebuilt. It meant a great deal to him that Yellow Spring boys and girls were getting a better education. His beliefs that the country was on course and the human race headed in the right direction had become articles of a strong secular faith.

Its erosion was probably, as is so often true, related to changing personal circumstances. His daughter Helen's death in 1980 and son Cornwell's a year later hit him very hard. As his eyes began to give out, making it hard for him to read, he sat in his chair worrying about his financial situation, which wasn't acute but had to be thought about. Unable to get down the cellar steps to work on his lathe or at his bench, he focused his increasing despair on the results of the 1980 national election. His faith in the order and direction of things, which had sustained the confidence that was part of his acceptance of age's attack, began to disappear.

As this happened, Mister Caudy turned increasingly to Faith's other dimension. I am poor witness to what formal religion meant to him; we recognized that we thought of theology in different terms, and he respected my difficulty with its institutionalized forms. We didn't talk much about religion.

I stumbled once, though, across the line he clearly held. His lamenting something that age was doing to one or another of his faculties reminded me of a suggestion I had made lightheartedly once in a speech: that life would make more sense lived the other way around. So that what is now the last and often burdensome part came first, followed by forty years or so of useful activity, then by a period concentrated on learning, and after that five or six years of tender loving care; with a doctor finally picking us up by the heels and patting us goodbye, instead of hello. Mister Caudy slapped his knee and laughed approvingly.

But instead of dropping the nonsense there, as I had in my speech, I milked it with the heathen musing that the Lord perhaps shouldn't have waited until the sixth day, when He was tired, to make human life. Mister Caudy stopped smiling. The rebuke came slowly and gravely. "No, Billie, He knows best."

Jane and I often found him reading his Bible, and when his eyesight dimmed, he got a large-print edition. He clearly found in it answers to his self-questioning that age had sharpened.

Caudy had adopted Ada's Dunkard orthodoxy when they were married. "She was devoted to her church. The Book says 'Change,' and knowing she couldn't, I did." After Ada's death, Mister Caudy joined the closer-to-home Christian Church up on Timber Ridge. He was an active, not just-on-Sundays, member.

When his hearing worsened, the congregation put in a system that connected a microphone at the pulpit to earphones at Mister Caudy's pew. This made him very happy. But several months later when a short in the circuit resulted in a sudden squeal that clearly couldn't be traced to either ministerial or celestial origin, he put the earphones down and never touched them again. He had his own line of communication to Headquarters. Religion was a central force for Caudy Davis, as it has always been for this community. It was a critical ingredient in his coming to terms with life's disillusioning sequence.

Mister Caudy's religious convictions emphasized doing as much as believing. We talked once, skirting our closed-off territory, about the antinomianism —counting faith alone enough to assure salvation —that Methodist circuit rider Francis Asbury found so virulent here two centuries ago. After a brief detour into the hazards of complicated words ("You don't find any in the Book"), Mister Caudy embraced the missionary's protest. "Too many people think it's enough if they bow their heads and say their prayers and sing hymns in church."

So if Pride and Independence were part of his formula and Faith was critically important, Mister Caudy was equally committed to continued Activity. With his future behind him, at least in any earthly sense, he recognized doing and thinking as ends in themselves. "I know I will wear out," he used to say, "but I won't rust out."

He worked intently as long as he could with his hands. We talked about how headwork doesn't let you know after you are through whether what you've done amounts to much; but when you make something with your hands you can tell whether it is good, just fair, or has to be done over.

In 1971, when he was eighty-five, Mister Caudy designed and diagrammed to one-sixteenth-of-an-inch accuracy two heavy-iron waterwheels, seven feet in diameter, which he then had made from his specifications. One wheel still turns in perfect balance down by the stream at the Capon Springs Hotel. The other is below our spring, near where the old Davis tannery used to stand. Several years later, when there was a problem with the basement pipes in his house, the man who refused to rust out handled most of the work on the pipes that did.

But physical doing wasn't enough. Being chairman of the bank board gave Caudy infinite satisfaction. The May 1984 meeting was one of only three or four that Chairman Davis missed in the eleven years of his incumbency. After a combination of pressure from the family and the sheriff finally forced him out of his Cadillac, his son Charles drove him to Gore for the board meetings and Roscoe Bowers, the bank president, brought him home. When the bank was moved to a new building, with the board room in the basement, a question arose about whether the elderly chairman could negotiate the stairway. The first time the passage was attempted, the president put a hand on the chairman's elbow—which froze the proceeding until the hand was removed.

Roscoe Bowers smiles when you ask him who really ran the board meetings. "I only prepared the agenda and provided the reports. Mister Caudy handled it from there. He knew Robert's Rules and stuck to them. There was no discussion before a motion had been seconded, or after one to table. Every detail had to be covered. The chairman wanted to be absolutely sure not only that the bank was right but that it would look right." The penny-conscious tax collector and the minute-sensitive surveyor were still at work.

Two other activities helped Caudy Davis feel younger than he was. As the years went on, he was happiest with a fishing rod in his hand. Our last trip was to Ruth Aikin's pond, on the old Kump place on Loman's Branch Road. Mister Caudy wasn't sure it was worth trying that day; the breeze was from the south, which he considered essential, but the moon was on the wane, which was bad. Jane and I, affected by the moon, got two or three small bluegills apiece. Mister Caudy breezed home on the south wind with eight or ten keepers.

That expedition paid another premium. When he asked where I had gotten the night crawlers, my confes-

sion that I had paid ten cents apiece for them at the
store left the old nimrod shaking his head sadly. "Your
front yard is full of them." I said I realized this but
hadn't learned how to approach the wigglers effectively. "All you need to do," he told me, "is soak the
ground in the evening. Then you connect two wires to
the prongs of an electric plug-in. Run one to a good
ground and another longer one to an eighteen-inch iron
rod. Stick the rod down in the wet yard and put the
plug into a socket. The electricity drives the worms
crazy and they come to the surface. Just go out and
start picking them up. You may have to switch the
connection on the plug."

Mister Caudy's other sustaining interest was politics. As long as his eyes permitted he read every word
about public affairs in the *Charleston Gazette* and the
Winchester Star, which he referred to resentfully as
"the advertisers" because they gave only superficial
coverage of what he wanted to know. The news stories
seemed to him to reflect more and more slippage in
national values and performance.

Caudy continued to be an ardent Democrat. Jane and
I went one evening during the 1980 West Virginia gu-
bernatorial campaign to a picnic that Jay and Sharon
Rockefeller gave for two thousand of the Democratic
faithful at the County Fairgrounds in Augusta. Mister
Caudy was there, and when the master of ceremonies,
State Senator Vernon Whitacre, introduced him as
"Mr. Democrat of Hampshire County," there was a
standing ovation. The even more memorable part of it
came afterward. Going down to congratulate both the
candidate and the patriarch, we found them together
with four or five other men in a small tent behind the
platform. Someone had put a fiddle in Mister Caudy's

hands, and as the others clapped the beat the ninety-four-year-old veteran sawed out "There'll Be A Hot Time in the Old Town Tonight." He apologized when he was through: "I've forgotten some of the notes, and I couldn't remember the key."

Despite our common mistake of saying thank you too late, this didn't happen to Caudy Davis. In addition to being named Outstanding West Virginian of the Year by Governor Rockefeller in 1980 (whether for his political seniority or his virtuosity on the violin), he was inducted not once but twice into the Order of the Thirty-Fifth Star, West Virginia's highest salute to those engaged over long periods of time in the thirty-fifth state's public affairs. He smiled when someone asked about the two certificates and medallions that hung side-by-side on his living room wall, testifying equally to statewide respect and to the Order's less-than-orderly record keeping. The first induction ceremony was on April 13, 1980. Mister Caudy dismissed that occasion lightly. "They gave away quite a few of them. It's only honorary."

But he was visibly affected when it happened again, on "Caudy Davis Day," March 6, 1983, at the Timber Ridge United Church. The West Virginia Secretary of State, James Manchin, was there, along with State Senator Vernon Whitacre and Delegate Daniel Shanholtz. An American flag was presented to the guest of honor as a salute to his son Sterling's sacrifice in World War II. Secretary Manchin's remarks in his unknowing re-induction of Mister Caudy into the Order of the Thirty-Fifth Star to which he already belonged were expansive. Senator Whitacre had trouble controlling his emotions as he traced the honoree's career. Mister

Caudy's own speech was appropriate for his ninety-seven years and for the gathering around him of as many friends and neighbors as the church could hold: "Goodness, gracious sakes alive." Exactly the right length, it said all the circumstances warranted.

Caudy Davis was denied the quick curtain he had earned. At ninety-eight, with virtually all physical and mental activity impossible, with independence lost but with instinctive pride intact, which made it harder, he went into a retirement home at Stephens City. Resisting at first, he eventually accepted the terms. He wore out, unrusted, on September 18, 1985, seven months before his hundredth birthday.

It is pleasant to think back to a conversation several years ago, when something was said about the variety of things Mister Caudy had done in his life. I asked why he had moved from teaching to milling, to politics and public service, to surveying. After a long hesitation, he responded slowly. "I'm not sure. Maybe part of it sometimes was having to. But there was more than that. Whenever I learned how to do something it didn't seem to interest me anymore. I got bored and wanted to try something else."

His answer to the next question, about what had been most gratifying, came quickly. "Being in the state assembly." That was the one enterprise he didn't have a chance to master.

In another conversation along a similar line, I mentioned the comment our handyman friend Charley Alger made once when he was helping us put the house in shape. "The only hard thing about any job is getting started." Jane had amended this to include "getting it finished," which Charley knew less about. Mister

Caudy disagreed with both of them. "The hardest part of any job," he said, "is doing it right." His lifelong trademark, this was his standard for growing old with grace and distinction.

I look out the window beside my desk again . . . see a figure walking along the edge of the woods at the base of the mountain . . . and let my mind blend the images of a young surveyor looking through his long glass and sighting his compass as he hurries into a nation's history . . . and of an older man, another surveyor, to whom Jane and I feel an equal, and closer, debt.

For the Affirmative

Sitting on the upstairs porch for a few minutes before supper, watching the bluebirds dive gracefully to the nest box on the post beside the apple tree, then looking down the pasture trimmed with Queen Anne's lace to the river and across to Fossil Hill, listening but hearing no sound except a bullfrog's twanging his bass viol over at the pond, we sometimes let ourselves slip into a reverie we know is a mistake. How much of its legacy will the valley be able to keep? For how long? When will timelessness run out on this little precinct of Almost Heaven?

Jane mentions that we see none of the killdeer we used to, and only occasional red-wing blackbirds. The barn swallows didn't renew their lease last year. The wildflower population has dwindled. I add something lugubrious about the malign weekend traffic along the road and the advertisements for "three-acre-or-smaller" lots that have gone up recently on the Ridge. We wonder how much the television aerials sprouting like thistles on the rooftops threaten homespun human values.

This could be only typical geriatric concern, two people getting older than is good for them, gratefully content with things as they are, worrying about whether their little world will change. But it's more than that.

The balance of nature problems are real enough. The killdeer and the swallows and the red-wing blackbirds probably left when their food supply dwindled because of the insecticides and pesticides that were brought in to improve the corn and wheat yields. We don't know what the side effects will be of having sprayed thousands of wooded acres with dimilin—to stop the ravages of the gypsy moth. The threat is that the oak trees will be lost, denuding the mountainside, destroying an important source of income, and depriving the deer of the acorns they live on.

But those are not the most serious problems. The question that gets larger and larger in everybody's mind is whether, and for how long, the valley can stay free of two infections. One is industrial development. The other is too many people.

A pair of recent experiences heighten these concerns. Although both of them turned out favorably, the warnings remain.

Four years ago, a stranger to the valley applied to the West Virginia Department of Natural Resources for a permit to open a strip sand mine on property he had recently purchased on Bear Garden Mountain, which faces the community of Capon Bridge and rises directly from the river. When a hearing on the application was held at the bridge, a hundred local residents were there to oppose it. A representative of mining interests in the state stood up and said to them: "You people better start facing facts. These mountains are full of high-grade sandstone. The glassmakers want this sand. Forget your 'aesthetics' and your canoers who don't like strip mines. We are going to get this sandstone."

The owner of the land pressed strongly for his right to use it as he wished and spoke of the additional jobs the mine would mean to the valley. His lawyer challenged the State Engineer, who was presiding at the hearing, to find any clearcut prohibition of the proposed operation in the West Virginia strip-mining law.

The application was denied. The threatened appeal of the decision was dropped.

The other experience, little known about but equally critical, involved another outsider's attempt in 1987 to purchase the 5,000 acres of land owned by the family that has operated the Capon Springs Hotel for fifty-five years. The hundreds of houses the prospective purchaser planned to build on that acreage would have been markers on the graves of what the valley has meant. The members of the hotel family, youthful stewards in their twenties and thirties, turned down an exceedingly lucrative offer, making it plain that the hotel's tradition—and the valley's—is not for sale.

But how long can this line be held? Property values in the valley are rising. Other owners may not be disposed or able to do what the hotel family did. One other substantial though smaller holding of valley land has been sold recently to a purchaser who is planning to cut it up. The glass industry continues to want the Oriskany sandstone, and the mining industry will never think highly of canoers and conservation-minded aesthetes.

I suspect that the valley's future hangs in a fairly close balance, and that the next two or three years will be critical. The question is whether the principle of community, which has a long history here, will be given the new force it is going to need.

I take the case for the affirmative.

This principle of community was put in simple words when a group of senior parishioners at Hebron Lutheran gathered one evening in July of 1986 in connection with the church's bicentennial preparations. They set out deliberately to draw from their memories and their experience the elements of this valley's essential character. They found themselves coming repeatedly to the phrase "caring and sharing"—and concluded that this is the combination of elements they were looking for.

Caring and sharing have a two-century history in the Capon Valley. My case for the affirmative rests on the belief that this brand of civic idealism will be given the muscle it needs to protect the valley's freedom from too many people and from their commercial-industrial pastimes.

This won't just happen. It will take joint action by the majority who love the valley against the few who don't care. There are enough signs of this unified action to warrant cautious hope.

The Capon Bridge sand-mine case had landmark significance. Those who were closest to the controversy realize that there were several reasons for the permit's denial. One was unquestionably pressure that was mobilized by two local citizen groups, the Capon Conservancy, organized at Capon Bridge to oppose the stripmine application, and the Capon River Committee, which had been established a few months earlier at Yellow Spring.

Karen Ripoli and Sarah Twigg, organizers of the Capon Conservancy, drew up a petition opposing the application and had it signed by every resident of Capon Bridge. This was filed with the Department of Natural Resources. Conservancy members then drove in force to Charleston, got in touch with state and federal legislative and executive offices, raised money to hire legal counsel, and then converged on the public hearing. The decision was considered a team victory.

The Capon River Committee, which joined effectively in the sand-mine opposition, had been organized to get the river cleaned up after the devastating hundred-year flood in 1985. The active founders included Jim Matheson, owner and operator of Camp Rim Rock; George Constantz, biology teacher at Hampshire High School; and Peggy Seldon and Willetta Davis, who trace their families back to eighteenth-century Capon Valley pioneers. A hundred residents of the area signed up quickly as members, and a treasury of over $3,000 was raised, most of it by small contributions.

The committee asked the Department of Natural Resources offices in Romney for help in clearing the river of the old stoves, refrigerators, used-tire carcasses, and fifty-foot logs that had piled up at critical points. Contacts were made with representatives in Charleston and Washington to arrange funding allocations. When Gary Morefoot from the DNR field office brought his well-equipped crew to the river in January of 1986 and stayed with them for the two weeks the clean-up job took, a new sense of the force of local initiative and government cooperation emerged in the valley.

After helping in the sand-mine case, the committee began moving on other fronts. It set up its own program to test regularly the quality of the Capon's water. When the gypsy moth invasion hit the valley, the committee organized the defense against it. The group has also maintained an active antilitter program.

Most of the committee programs have been triggered by crisis: the flood, the threat to scar the valley with a strip mine, the invasion by hordes of fuzzy insects with insatiable appetites for oak leaves and with the capacity for loathsome multiplication. Community action, more easily mustered when an enemy enters the valley, is harder to mobilize for defenses against threats that have only begun to materialize. But a broader agenda is being developed.

George Constantz has established a laboratory to do the river testing and has worked out a proposal for the permanent monitoring of all changes in the river's ecosystem that might threaten its future. If his efforts succeed, the Capon will have a full-time, scientifically trained, dedicated ombudsman.

The CRC land use subcommittee is working on another critical set of defense measures. No zoning regulations, except for a dead-letter Wardensville ordinance, protect the river basin. Subdivision ordinances adopted in Morgan County and under consideration in Hampshire establish only minimal restrictions. Planning commissions set up in these two counties are moving slowly and without any special regard for the valley's particular interests. The danger of an influx of people or commerce or industry increases daily.

Steps are being taken toward the development of land-use policies for the valley. Knowing that the only effective programs will be those that have wide-based local support, the CRC has prepared, with member Nancy Ailes's special help, a Capon Valley land register that will include the names and addresses of the fifteen-hundred valley property holders. The register

will be used as a basis for soliciting local property owners' views about appropriate land-use policies and to
muster citizen support for implementing agreed-upon
measures.

I think of Alexis de Tocqueville coming to this country in the early nineteenth century and concluding that
the essential element of *Democracy in America* is the
custom of depending on people working together, with
little reliance on laws or formal government, to do
whatever needs to be done. This sense and spirit of
community, including but going beyond nature's conservancy, are alive and working along the Cacapon.

When the women at Hebron or Christian Church or
the Rod and Gun Club have their turkey-and-ham or
oyster suppers every few weeks, the dining room is full
and people line up at the door. You feel that you have
dropped in on a big family get-together.

The Local Ruritan Club, lively and vital, has recently bought a ten-acre plot on River Road for a park
and has put up there an attractive picnic shelter. At
its first annual Fourth of July pig roast in 1988 so
many people came that the barbecued pork and homemade ice cream were gone within an hour. Sitting with
two hundred neighbors on the benches under the shelter, listening to a talented local gospel singer and to
the Ruritan String Band strumming out first-rate
country and folk classics, gave us more genuine Fourth
of July spirit than we have felt since we were kids.

When the younger Yellow Spring men decided to put
together a softball team, they did it so well and hung
together so effectively that they worked their way
twice to state and national tournaments. Needing cash
for expenses, they barbecued three hundred chicken
halves, which were sold off immediately. The players'

wives and their friends fielded another team that was as good in its league as the men's. And better watching.

In the spring of 1988, the state road authorities checked the old bridge at Capon Lake and put up a sign restricting it to three-ton loads, which cripples its traffic. Three-hundred-and-fifty people turned out for the emergency meeting that was held at the hotel. A petition was drawn up. The bridge got moved from the bottom of the state priority list to the top, and will be replaced in 1990 or 1991.

I don't know whether this valley, only a hundred miles from two large cities, will be able to ward off the infection of urban sprawl. I don't know for sure whether people whose families have depended on the land and the river for generations can accept sufficiently the fact that the land and the river now depend on people. The tradition in the valley is that land is part of the person who owns it. The new question is whether this can be extended to include the idea of the land and river being part of the community, so that the community binds together to prevent losing the land and river—and itself.

I do know that there is an extraordinary sense here of caring and sharing, and that the sharing includes a willingness to join in exercising crucial responsibility. This is enough for me. As the years add up, I find increasing good sense in falling back, when cold reason doesn't take me all the way I want to go, on faith. I am reasonably confident, at least in my heart, that in this enthralling valley, where the human purpose remains cradled in nature's special kindness, the future will continue to be a good idea.

Credits And Creditors

Part of the pleasure of doing the Sampler has been the interweaving of different kinds of thread: scraps of hearsay legend, gleanings from family genealogies, items from cookbooks and a cobbler's ledger, and then the little bit about the valley that has gotten into public print, especially the local newspaper. So a customary bibliography would be inappropriate. I'll simply note, along with an acknowledgement of the very large debts I owe a number of people, the relatively few published sources that are reflected here.

I have leaned cautiously, usually with attribution, on what are recognized locally as classics: Samuel Kercheval's *History of the Valley of Virginia*, which first appeared in 1833; Hu Maxwell's and H.L. Swisher's *History of Hampshire County* (1897); and Maud Pugh's two-volume *The Capon Valley: It's [sic] Pioneers and Their Descendants* (1946 and 1948). Respect for these works is so widespread that any protest about their being anecdotal and disorganized would diminish the complaint more than the classic. My only real grievance is that they mention Yellow Spring, if at all, only in passing. *Historic Hampshire*, edited in 1976 by Selden W. Brandon, should also be noted.

So far as the sketch of early Capon Valley land titles and George Washington's surveying goes beyond J.M. Toner's editing of Washington's 1748 *Journal,* it relies for basic information on several standard works: Washington Irving, *Life of George Washington* (3 Vol. 1855); Rupert Hughes, *George Washington, The Human Being and the Hero* (1926); William Couper, *History of the Shenandoah Valley* (5 Vol., 1952); Douglas Southall Freeman, *George Washington* (1948). The more interesting and illuminating details come from various publications of the Winchester-Frederick County Historical Society: Oren Frederic Morton's monograph, *The Story of Winchester in Virginia* (1925); a 1974 report by Garland R. Quarles, *George Washington and Winchester, Virginia*; and an undated pamphlet published by the Society entitled *Historic Winchester and the Shenandoah Valley of Virginia*. Philander D. Chase's illuminating monograph, *A Stake in The West, George Washington as Backcountry Surveyor and Landholder,* is based on his address at a conference at Shenandoah College in Winchester in April, 1989.

The tracing of Yellow Spring roots comes primarily from several family genealogies: Albert Thompson Secrest's *Spaid Genealogy* (1922); Robert E. Reid's *Reid Family, Jeremiah Reed of Timber Ridge* (1959, available in mimeographed form in the Capon Bridge Public Library); *L'Histoire de la Famille La Follette en Amerique*, published by Franklin LaFollette Jones in 1972; *Brumbach:Hotsinpillar Genealogy*, edited in 1961 by Elizabeth Chapman Denny Vann and Margaret Collins Senny Dixon; Joseph Harvey Vance's, *The Vance Family Scrapbook* (1970). Charles Brill, of Gore, gave me the details regarding his family, and Barbara Hahn of Wardensville, who is developing a rich depository of valley history, provided a number of genealogical items.

The Davis family history, which I have drawn on so heavily, is set out in two forms. Lillian Virginia (Ludwig) Davis published a genealogy of the *William Davis Family* (William was Samuel Davis's brother) in 1972. John and Dorothy (Davis) Holleran have prepared a meticulous and thorough genealogy, still in typescript form, of the Samuel Davis line, including the histories of the families (most of those in the Yellow Spring part of the valley) the Davises have married into.

Grace Kelso Garner and Ralph L. Triplett have done the most extensive surveying of Eastern Hampshire County and Western Frederick County genealogical records. The copy I found of their jointly prepared (and mimeographed) *Early Births, Western Frederick County, Virginia* is undated. Garner's *Earliest Settlers, Western Frederick-Eastern Hampshire Counties* was issued in mimeographed form in 1978. The four volumes of the Triplett recording of markers in Hampshire County cemeteries appeared in typescript in 1974.

The Sampler is based to a considerable extent on conversations with people in Yellow Spring. Quite a bit of what is here came from Caudy and Forrest Davis, who were unbelievably patient in the dozens of casual talks we had together. Caudy's sons, Charles and Sam, and his daughter, Sylvia Forrester, added a lot, including pictures of their father and mother. I borrowed Sam's copy of Lawrence P. Winnemore's 1975 story of *The Winchester and Western Railroad*. Forrest's brother Frank salted and peppered several sections with his apt anecdotes, and Frank's wife Etta found some important Davis family pictures.

I owe a large debt to Ben and Elizabeth Frye. In addition to providing numerous leads to invaluable informational sources, they took the trouble to read carefully an earlier draft of the Sampler and to offer friendly suggestions about it. They could and should do for Wardensville what I have tried to do for Yellow Spring; the Fryes and the Wardens deserve being told about.

Ruth Rudolph opened up the history of the Hebron Lutheran Church, and Norman Walker helped enliven the Tilbury Orndorff story. Benson LaFollette made World War I quietly vivid, and a morning with Armetha Haines Carrier was a lesson in what the teachers in one-room schoolhouses could accomplish—and what they couldn't. Charles Anderson drew from his remarkable memory dozens of details that I didn't have before, and straightened out a number of others that I had wrong. Genevieve (Miller) Watson gave me most of the Kline information and helped me understand some family and regional history she knows thoroughly.

Bonni McKeown, from the Capon Springs Hotel, has taped a number of interviews with older Capon Hollow residents. I have barely touched on the rich stories they tell, assuming and hoping tht Bonni will put them together in her own delightful style.

Calvin Kytle, the recently retired president and publisher of Seven Locks Press, went far beyond any obligation that might flow from our years of working together; reading an early draft, he told me bluntly that it missed its mark, but encouraged doing it differently. Jack Gentry, going to the same trouble, was lighter in his criticism and heavier on the encouragement, which was equally helpful. Our friends and neighbors Anne Queneau and Jim Megronigle are meticulously careful readers, sensitive editors, and constructive critics.

Kathleen Ferguson Jump, a talented editor, managed in her gracious way to break me, at least partially, from some habits that writing as a lawyer, pedagogue, and bureaucrat had engrained. Donnali Fifield, skilled and sensitive, assumed responsibility for the final editing and improved what is here as far as a stubborn author permitted.